Tales from
the West Pole

A Dreamer's Uncharted Journey

Marylu Downing

Tales from the West Pole: A Dreamer's Uncharted Journey
© 2013 by Marylu Downing

ISBN: 978-0615892160

Cover images: Marylu Downing
Cover design and logo: Jennifer Beckham
Book design: Jo-Anne Rosen

All interior photos and illustrations are the work of the author, except as noted below.
© Marylu Downing 2013

Some art work based on originals by others:

- Picture of Roger House and Marylu Downing—manipulated photo from an original by Susan Morris
- Picture of Play the Blues at our Wedding—manipulated photo from an original by Debbie Davis
- Picture of I'm An Artist Now—manipulated version from an original photo by Weymouth Kirkland
- Picture of the Union Hotel—manipulated image from their website archives
- Picture of Gerry Schultz and Marylu Downing taken at Camp Meeker in a photo booth
- Picture of Victorian Shirt—manipulated G. Shields illustration for Folkwear Patterns
- Picture of Christo Fence—manipulated from a photo on Internet archives
- Picture of Dancing Woman—manipulated from an original photo by Laurel Kirkland

Additional credits:

- "Music from Home," words by Marcy Telles, score by Gordon Stubbe for the Occidental Community Choir
- "Songbird," first published in *Tiny Lights*, 2007
- "Snake Creeps Down," first published in Copperfields' *The Dickens*, 2001
- "Tap Dancing Birthday Cake," first published in *Wordrunner eChapbooks*, 2013

To see color versions of the images in this book, go to www.studioml.com.

Naked Lady Publications

Freestone, California

This book is dedicated to the belief in love, compassion,
and the existence of magical places on the earth
that will always stay nearly the same.

To my family, and to all the people
living at the West Pole.

With special thanks to Roger F. House
for his efforts in helping me
create the material for this book,
in every way possible.

About the Book

This is a work of creative non-fiction. It is purely subjective and dependent on a perhaps faulty memory. Nevertheless, it's related to living my life in a particular place at a particular time, and I've given it my best shot. Out of kindness, many names have been changed to protect the innocent, and the not so innocent.

Marylu Downing, September 2013, West Pole

Chinese Proverb

You cannot prevent the birds of sorrow
from flying over your head,
but you can refuse to let them
build their nests in your hair.

Discovering the West Pole

A couple, lost and befuddled on the Bohemian Highway, drove into a small northern California town. The first thing they saw was a disheveled version of Santa Claus raking leaves.

The woman rolled down the car window, looked at the man known as Ranger Rick, and asked, "Where in the world are we?"

Ranger stopped raking, put his hands on top of his rake handle, and rested his chin on his hands. Looking up at a blue, blue sky, Rick said, "Well, ye have landed at the West Pole." Ranger nodded and smiled and went back to keeping the town sparkling clean.

Contents

Tales from the West Pole:

A Dreamer's Uncharted Journey

Recipe

Let it begin with
garlic cloves,
thin angel hair pasta,
salted water set to boil.

Side by side
another pan
filled with tomatoes
straight from the earth.
Add a bay laurel leaf just
plucked from the tree outside.

Boil noodles until the water
bubbles, practically hoots,
like the owls calling to
each other in the redwood night.

Stir the tomatoes,
the spices.
Garlic wrinkles the air.

Then bowl up
the noodles
like a bird's pale nest.
Cover with thick,
warm sauce and DIG IN

A Love Affair

The San Andreas Fault, the Ring of Fire, the tidal tug of the Pacific Ocean—that's my comfort zone. A native Californian, I yearn to try something new, move on, find a new horizon line. In my search for just the right place I've fallen in love over and over again. Sometimes a potent aroma draws me in, or the full moon at fall harvest time when it looks like a big round Chinese lantern hanging in the sky. It could be as simple as wood smoke curling up from a campfire, or the way dirt feels as it sifts through my fingers. I long to rearrange reality, capture fleeting moments in a painting or in a dream.

As with most love affairs, this one starts innocently enough with a phone call from Will, a friend of my husband Scott. I don't know this friend Will yet. It's 1972 and Scott and I are newly married and just getting to know each other.

Will calls from a pay phone; he practically yells, "You've got to get up here and see this place! Tell Scott to drive you and the kids up here. We'll wait for you at this Italian joint called The Union Hotel in Occidental. I'm telling you, this doesn't even seem like it's in America!" He shouts goodbye and hangs up.

I walk over to our bed in the laundry room and reach over to shake Scott awake. In addition to my daughter, five-year-old Gracie, we have our eight-month-old baby, Mary Lea. We're buying and remodeling a wreck of an old 1920s house in Mill Valley. We are sleep deprived and catch naps when and where we can.

"Your friend Will just called. He says to come to a place called Occidental."

"What time is it?" Scott asks.

"It's about 3:30 in the afternoon, and in case you're wondering, it's still Sunday."

"Okay," Scott says, rolling out from under the blankets, "let's do it. I don't know where in hell it is, but we'll find the place, and it'll be a break from all this work."

He stretches and yawns as Mary Lea stirs in her crib in the dining room. We don't yet have a living room. The place is tiny, but has its charms. What was once the living room has been turned into a country kitchen with a small fireplace, and the walls are shingled on the inside so the whole place smells of cedar.

"I agree; we need some fun." I love Italian food; I'm starting to salivate.

Scott pulls on his jeans, puts on a flannel shirt, gets a map out of our VW camper and marks a route through the back country, cutting over at Petaluma into Western Sonoma County, and then on to our final destination, Occidental, about an hour north of us. I've dressed the girls and put together a diaper bag. Grace picks out some favorite books and her crayons and paper. We're ready.

"I've heard of the place—it's where the Wheeler Ranch is," I say, "and it's where that author I love, Alicia Bay Laurel, lives. I just bought her book, *Living on the Earth*. The place is hippie commune country." I'm smiling because I'm quietly attracted to the whole hippie flower-power movement, but really haven't acted on it much except to repair my jeans and Mary Lea's stroller with patches of colorful embroidered cloth or leather. And I do smoke the occasional joint.

"What?" Scott looks up from the map. He doesn't really know what I'm talking about. He just wants to meet up with his hometown Chicago buddy, Will, and Will's girlfriend Sandra. They're fresh out of the Peace Corps, just returning to America after several years in Ecuador. Scott was recently discharged from the Navy where he was posted to Japan. His minesweeper went into the waters near Vietnam many times. I left a good job as a social worker, and said goodbye to my family in Corona del Mar, a Southern California beach community. I happily turned my back on life as a single mom and remarried, started a new family. There's been a tidal shift for all of us.

The quality of light this time in the late afternoon on a Northern California fall day makes the pastoral landscape seem almost out of a Vermeer painting, but the subject matter—the sheared sheep, the black and white cows—seem foreign to us suburban dwellers. We wind around country roads crossing through the backside of Petaluma and into sleepy Two Rock and then Valley Ford, past smooth rounded hills fading to brown. Sheep graze intently, their noses poked into the dry grasses.

I breastfeed baby Mary Lea as we drive. Five-year-old Grace colors for awhile, and then wants to know, "When are we going to get there?"

Sheep ranches with Swiss names, *Straus, Dolcini, Luchessi* on the mailboxes, and dairy ranches with Portuguese names, *Matos, Bordessa, Santos, Cardoza,* and Italian names, *Francheschi, Alberigi,* dot the Bodega Highway landscape. When we round the final bend in the road and turn left onto Bohemian Highway, everything changes. We've entered the forest with its enchantments, redwoods creating a tunnel as we drive the final stretch.

When we come up the last rise, Occidental appears.

"Quaint," I say.

"Tiny," Scott says.

"And magical. Like Brigadoon, maybe we'll never leave." I say.

Only two blocks long, the town is filled with white clap-board houses from the early 1900s, and tucks into a saddle point between two hills covered in madrone, tan oak, and redwood. Bits of wispy fog cling to the tops of the trees.

Scott maneuvers the VW camper into a spot in front of the hotel, and we look at each other and smile. We like the place; we're not sorry for the effort it's taken to get here. To our surprise, the town is filled with cars. There are three Italian family-style restaurants to choose from. Throngs of tourists file in to dine, soaking up the local color and the local flavors of the place.

As we open the car doors to take the girls out of the back, the air smells of summer camp—of fir, woodsmoke and garlic. We wait for three long-haired young women in ankle length flowered skirts balancing babies on their hips, to walk by before going into the Union Hotel. Scott stares after the young

women wistfully while roosters crow from somewhere just out of sight. The town is surrounded by an overwhelmingly natural beauty, redwood trees climbing up the hills as far as I can see. The red spire of a Catholic church stands out against green trees, complimentary colors. The artist in me says, "Yes!"

It takes a few minutes for my eyes to adjust to the dark of the high-ceilinged Union Hotel, built, as the sign outside proudly proclaims, in 1879. The long dimly-lit dining halls are filled with tables covered in red checkered cloths, and the walls are hung with fading photographs of the Italian founders, the Gonellas and the Panizzeras.

"There they are," my husband Scott says, running over to give friend Will a big bear hug. We introduce all around. Sandra, with her head of long, curly dark hair takes wiggly baby Mary Lea while Gracie and I head for the bathroom. The bathroom is filled with freshly cut stems of lavender, a clever natural deodorizer. When we come back, everyone sits at a long wooden table with friendly strangers, in traditional Italian family-style dining. It feels like some of our favorite places on Columbus Street in San Francisco's North Beach.

We proceed to eat the largest dinner of our lives: Antipasto of kidney beans and salami, mozzarella and peppers followed by salad, a big pot of minestrone soup, bread, followed by handmade raviolis, spaghetti, baked chicken, and Gracie's favorite, a dessert of apple fritters dusted with sugar and cinnamon. We groan and take our bagged-up leftovers into the saloon, with its old hand-carved wooden bar, colorful bottles gleaming in the smoky, hazy light. It's almost dark out now, but we aren't ready to leave the feel-good of the place. The hotel seems ripe for love. Even the menu describes how love blossomed when waitress Mary Alberigi fell down the stairs from the second floor and was swooped up into the arms of the hotel owner, Carlo Panizzerra. He carried her to the doctor and on the way fell in love. They married shortly afterwards, starting a dynasty of Italian restaurateurs. We're warmed by the glow of the place as we sit listening to accordion music. The bartender tells us the blind accordion player, Emil Bordi, is almost ninety years old.

Grace makes friends with some other kids, and they all dance around to the jumpy music. I feel a tug, a yearning, an immediate kinship with this town, with its unspoiled Italian atmosphere, its casual, friendly environment. As untraveled as I am at the age of 31 it seems like a mini trip to Europe. I relax for the first time in months. In Mill Valley it seems that everyone we know is a film director, a commercial artist, a rock star, or a famous author. For the first time, I'm a stay-at-home mom—one with a carpenter's belt, new baby slung on her back, stacks of lumber and other building supplies piled up in the yard. I might stroll to town with Graham Nash or nod to Jerry Garcia at the market, but I live in a world where Scott and I sleep in a make-shift bedroom in the tiny laundry room with walls I've decoupaged in cleverly-drawn black and white Macy's newspaper ads from the *San Francisco Chronicle*. There is only one bedroom, which has no closet, but a used bunk bed which now holds Grace and will soon hold Mary Lea. Mill Valley is a town filled with people who believe in the concept of Zero Population Growth and the elementary schools are closing. This Occidental seems to be populated with, actually, overflowing with, babies.

"What's wrong?" Will asks.

I'm crying a little,

"I want to live here. This is the place for me," I say, turning to Scott.

A funny look crosses my husband's face. "What! You want to leave Mill Valley? We just moved there. You thought that was your place." He hasn't caught on to me yet, doesn't know about the Tarot deck with the Magician, the Hangman, the Fool.

"Well, now I've seen this place, I'm in love," I say.

Grace wraps her arms around me, "Don't cry, Mommy."

"I'm fine," I say, "I'm not really sad."

And it's true. Sometimes love is that way. Like crying at weddings. Some part of you has been touched, some sentimental button pushed. It's that moment when you realize there's no turning away from love and you're not sure you even want to be in love.

We say goodbye to Will and Sandra. Outside, the skies, unhampered by city lights, are lit by what seem a million stars. I feel like I'm in that Georgia O'Keefe painting of the huge gnarly tree, *The Lawrence Tree,* branches reaching up and up to a star-filled night. I tuck the girls into the camper bed and Grace throws a protective arm across her little sister. Both girls sleep all the way home. It's very quiet in the car on the way back. We can't find a topic, don't know what to say to each other. A door has opened. A new possibility looms as large as the redwood trees.

That night as I climb over Scott to get into my side of the bed, which is shoved up against the wall so that there is still room to walk into the house I say, "Something about that place, I think I want to move there. Eventually," I carefully add.

"No, I don't even want to think about it!" Scott grumbles, turning his back and putting a pillow over his head.

"Goodnight."

"Goodnight."

I close my eyes but don't sleep. Towering trees cast shadows. In the distance owls hoot, calling to each other. Entering the forest, I feel the soft uneven redwood duff beneath my bare feet. I see my ancestor, Admiral Byrd, explorer of the North Pole look down at a compass. I peek over his shoulder. The spinning dial stops on the "W." It points due west—to the Occident, to the West Pole.

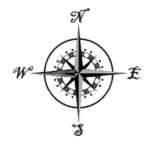

Cathedral

In winter,
trees glisten silver
at the tips
reflecting back
car headlights.
Small increments,
new growth,
that when gathered
together make a giant,
and several giants make
a fairy circle,
a cathedral with spires to the sky.

An Air Stream and a Tool Belt

"How many people live here, anyway?" neighbors ask as they walk by our Mill Valley remodel. They're afraid the neighborhood has been invaded by hippies. First my parents arrived pulling a little house trailer behind their car which they stay in while they help us begin the addition. As soon as they left, Will and Sandra came. They parked their truck with its turtle's home of a camper shell in our driveway, ready to help me work on the house while Scott goes to work in San Francisco.

Right away, just like they did when they were teenagers in Chicago, Will and Scott get into trouble together. One night Sandra and I have to bail them out of jail. When Will calls, Sandra drives over with the money. The boys who were now men, had been parked in their vehicles in a residential area. Nothing is directly said, but it is implied they had company in their cars. Women.

Scott and Will are gone a lot of nights, often to play chess at the No Name Bar in Sausalito, a notorious hang out for porn stars. Sandra and I are left to clean up messes and put the girls to bed. Sometimes when he comes home Scott smells strongly of Patchouli oil, and it's not his.

Will adopts a mangy, kind of scary German Shepherd which sleeps in their truck. The dog snarls anytime anyone comes over. It's bitten a friend of ours and I worry that the dog may attack the kids. Eventually I say to Scott that Will must leave the driveway haven for some other place. I don't care where. I will miss the good natured company and excellent cooking of Sandra, but not her boyfriend Will.

About this time, our Mill Valley friends, Maria and Joe and their children, move to Occidental. They live in a mobile home and start building a house. We regularly drive up to visit and often end up at the Union Hotel for a bite to eat. Once again, the same old guy, Emil, even older now, plays Italian music in the saloon. Each time we leave to return to our little Marin County house, I'm left with a deep longing. I know Occidental is my spot on planet earth.

One day we drive north to see the Christo Running Fence along the back roads between Marin and Sonoma counties. It flaps in the wind, the white nylon panels looking like sails of a ship as it climbs across the hills. It's a beauty and it makes me feel even more bonded to the country, to the area of the west county which Jeanne Claude and her husband Christo chose to accentuate with their installation art. It is a watershed moment for me as soon as I see it.

When we get home, I say to Scott, "I'm moving up there; you can come if you want to."

"What! Are you crazy? We live in paradise!" he says.

"It's your paradise now, not mine."

Scott shakes his head in amazement, but he knows he owes me a favor. There have just been too many woman nicknamed Susie Cream Cheese in his life here.

"Okay, okay," he says a while later, "make a plan." He sees the Fool's determination on my face. He knows the look now.

The next day I start a folder with pictures from magazines. I rip out pages with houses and gardens that I think are pretty or that use passive solar energy to heat and cool. Facing southwest is the best way to go in California. I start dreaming, planning, scheming my move.

A few months after this decision to move, our friend Joe spots a great piece of property for sale, six acres facing southwest. He has a phone number from the ad in the local Sonoma County newspaper for us to call. We drive up again, this time without the kids, and take a look. It seems like a state park to me and I break down crying because I can't believe individuals can own a place like this. I'm intimidated, but like a woman considering taking up with a man who seems out of reach, I fall in love anyway, and there's no way to stop the pursuit. It will be ours. We've improved our Mill Valley house for seven years and it's in a great neighborhood, walkable into town, so we should get enough to pay for the land, and build a house. Land's cheaper in Sonoma County.

Dad's a realtor, and he helps us arrange to buy the acreage, contingent on the sale of our Mill Valley home. We list our house with its decoupaged laundry/bedroom, used brick patio I'd laid down in a herringbone pattern, and the six pairs of French doors Dad carted on the top of his truck from Southern California which are now part of the great room addition. We're inundated on the first day it's listed for sale, and by dinner time, we accept an offer. The realtor for our house is the father of a Mill Valley musician from *Quicksilver Messenger Service,* John Cippolino. The town is just filled with rockers and families of rockers.

A few weeks later, we leave Mill Valley for the West Pole. I drive the camper with the two girls, two cats and our golden retriever. Scott drives a U Haul with everything else. By mistake I leave all my childhood collections, scrapbooks, and old recipe books behind in the house's 1920s garage. The same garage our neighbors petitioned to have condemned as an "eyesore."

We're relocating 60 miles north. We hope to build our dream house, complete with a fix up for our faltering marriage.

We leave behind the grueling Dipsea Trail, which Scott loves to run. We leave friends and school enrichment programs and Mountain Theater plays on Mt. Tam. We leave behind an easy drive into the city and buses that can take us almost anyplace, and all the marital misadventures and open marriage proponents, to head for the simple country life.

Dad warned me as he left, "Building a house can wreck a marriage. I know," he continued, "I've seen it many times." He'd been a Southern California building contractor. He suggested that I be the "owner builder" and he'll advise me over the phone. We can save a lot of money that way. I agree to be the contractor, but what I don't say is that our marriage is already in trouble, so we feel we have nothing to lose by building a house.

After spending time watching the sun's patterns on the land and finding the way the wind always blows in from off the ocean, we choose a building site. We mark chalk lines for a driveway and hire a water witcher to help us place the well. We need to find water before we can get a building permit. The land had already passed its percolation test for the septic system, but it's 1977, a drought year. We must discover close to two gallons of water a minute to dig a well and get our permits.

Scott and the water witcher he hires, a tall bearded redhead, drink whiskey from a flask and smoke a joint together as they seek the special spot for our well. The area they pick is in the center of the road leading to our house.

When Dad returns from meeting with the realtor, he says "You've picked a place in the road easement and it won't do! You'll have to find another spot!" I can tell he is mad and probably frustrated with our lack of knowledge and our impulsive decision making, not to mention the crazy behavior of our water witcher and Scott too.

Whiskey and pot have mellowed the water witcher to the point where he can't make the metal wires cross over each other anywhere on the property now so he justs puts a stake on a random spot near the top of the property and calls it a day, lighting up another joint.

The well driller with his rusted and noisy equipment arrives, and for two days we listen to the churning of an auger grinding down through the earth, each layer of sediment examined and cataloged. At about 60 feet down, muddied water comes splashing out the top of the pipe. It's a Eureka moment and we all scream ourselves hoarse. Water, at least two gallons a minute, means we have enough to meet Sonoma County's building requirement. The water isn't good; it's filled with iron, smells of rotten eggs, and later on stains the bathroom and kitchen fixtures a rusty red color, but now we can truly begin on our dream house, our dream life.

Scott buys an old pick-up truck and uses it to bring in the water storage tank we'd bought as a mass of redwood planks that resembles a giant jigsaw puzzle. It takes hours to fit the redwood tank together, but it works, and soon water flows into it.

We take down third-growth redwood trees for the building site, and hire logger Bob Maddocks to cut and haul the trees for milling. Maddocks uses a crane to load his truck until it's full to the brim and we watch the truck wobble out the drive and list down pot-holed Deer Meadow Lane. He'll have to twist around several curvy roads to get to Rico Calvi's one-man lumber mill. Soon we have milled redwood which we will use for shelving. We think it's very cool that our own trees become wood to use in our own house. We're still getting used to the idea of owning redwoods.

We plan to tile the house, hang the doors and windows, shingle it, put on the trim and paint the interior ourselves, but we hire subcontractors for all the things we can't or don't want to do. This is during the height of the back-to-the-land movement and, like a lot of others, we wear our tough brown leather Santa Rosa work boots and have suede leather carpenter's belts slung over our cut-off jeans. I've been able to incorporate some of my dream folder ideas into the plans a friend draws up, but the project has to be scaled back. The upstairs art studio and guest room will just sit as a large attic for now. The garage also has to be put on hold. Despite these restrictions, the dream house seems just right for us. It's slightly larger than the old place, and when it's finished, there will be closets and individual bedrooms for the girls.

An artistic friend brings us a couple of three-dimensional stained glass windows. He has removed them in the middle of the night from a San Francisco bar that never paid him for his work. He sells them to us at a discounted price and suggests we use them in the front bathroom. They will let in light, but the color will still provide privacy. The building site is starting to resemble the old Mill Valley place with piles of lumber, saw horses, buckets of nails, boxes of screws, shovels, and varying lengths and colors of plastic pipe.

For days I'm down in a trench gluing together pipe for leach lines, or on the phone soothing a sheet rocker who must be moved down on the schedule. I'm getting a taste of what it's been like for Dad all these years. I have a shouting match with the framing contractor, who refuses to take direction from a "clueless woman." The phone guy won't install the lines and poles, "until there's a man on the job I can talk to." I call Scott to come home so that this problem of phone lines can be resolved. The whole exchange with the phone guy sends me out into the woods to hike off my anger.

We hire another branch of the Calvi family, a legendary father/son operation, to bulldoze and shale a long circular driveway. As soon as it's finished, Scott drives an old 40-foot Air Stream trailer onto the land. We hook up electricity to the trailer, move from a rental in Camp Meeker and the Air Stream becomes our temporary home. We all inspect the trailer, with its bunk beds, bathroom, compact closets, the table that folds down at night into our bed. A fancy form of camping. The girls decide to call it Hi Ho Silver. They've always loved giving nick-names to people and things.

It's exhilarating to wake up in Hi Ho Silver to a mix of bird-song and the buzz of saws. As the walls go up, and the roof sheeting goes on, Scott and I make an agreement. I'll help staple on the roof shingles but I plan to shingle the bottom half of the house and Scott will do the top. I've never been fond of heights and I've just finished seven years of this top of the ladder work and climbing around on shaky scaffolding in Mill Valley. "I'm done with scaffolds," I tell Scott.

With the green thumb help of Occidental Hardware's Louis Gonella, we plant a large vegetable garden, and like most of our neighbors, we're soon gardening in the nude. I feel a little awkward at first, but with all this newfound privacy, after a few days, it seems perfectly comfortable to be planting corn, putting up strings for beans, or packing dirt around tomato plants *au naturel*. Sometimes all I have on are my gardening gloves. In this day before sunscreen, we are as brown as berries.

We begin to participate in our community. The girls attend Harmony School in town. They have a long hike through the forest to the bus stop down on Bittner Road, so we have to get up extra early. I'm teaching tap dancing and an exercise class at our small community center and working in an art enrichment program after school. I have a sometime job as a tap dancing cake for a telegram company in Marin County. I'm still making quirky objects for a gallery in Sausalito. I don't have time for a regular job yet, but I hear about a couple of part-time jobs I can interview for later on. Building always costs more than you plan for, even though you plan for it!

We're invited to potlucks and volleyball parties and quickly arranged barbecues at nearby Doran Beach, only a 15-minute drive west. We start to fit in, to tuck into our new town.

We run a temporary hookup from the septic system to the trailer and are now able to use the bathroom in Hi Ho Silver. But the shower doesn't offer much. Neighbors invite us to have hot showers at their houses or come over for a hot tub soak. We're getting cozy now. We're exploring our six acres, and our town. The girls find small black arrowheads at the bottom of the property. Grace thinks it's an old sacred spot. They ride their bikes on the lane and come back with blackberries, still hot from the sun. We cook pies in our second hand O'Keefe and Merrit oven. Scott makes a special study of the three bars in town and the bar maids.

Gonella's Market, the grocery store downtown, holds our UPS packages for us, but for months we don't know this. One day the owner asks, "Do you live up on the lane? If you do, I think we've got a package for you. Did you order something from Macy's? It's a big box."

"Yes, I ordered new pillows and sheets." I feel a need to prove the package is mine by saying what's in it. "But that was about a month ago!"

He goes on to explain that the delivery trucks won't go on our dirt lane. In winter it's a river and too steep, too filled

with pot holes. It wreaks havoc on their trucks and re-dis-
tributes their loads. "Just come by here if you're expecting a
package." And for the next few years we do.

I'm invited to be a part of a vaudeville show at the Camp
Meeker Players. They think the cake job means I'm an enter-
tainer. It takes a while before they understand I don't jump
out of a cake naked, but dance inside a cake costume. A local,
Gerry Schultz, invites me to sing with her. She chooses the
song, "All for the Best," from Godspell. We're dressed in angel
costumes I've made and we wear classic dyed yellow mops for
hair and have gauzy blue wired wings safety pinned on, with
slide whistles around our necks. I am nervous just before the
curtain goes up.

"Do you feel that shaking?" Gerry asks. We are back to back
on stage. "Are we having an earthquake?"

"It's me. Stage fright," I say, "I'll be all right once the music
starts."

"Oh, I've never had stage fright," she says, hands in prayer
pose as the curtain lifts.

In the audience I see the brothers from the hardware store, the people who own Gonella's Market, our neighbors and new friends, among lots of unfamiliar faces. I just keep singing and dancing until finally, blissfully, it's over. Curtain down. My parents have come for the show and they've enjoyed the whole thing. It reminds them of the "good old days in the San Fernando Valley."

After gray Mill Valley, the sunshine on our property feels so good that I sit out on the little deck by the trailer and sew. Once on a very hot day, I'm sewing without a stitch on, and get caught by a carpenter. "Whoops," he says as he turns slowly to walk back to the building site. We are getting pretty casual in our new lifestyle. In some ways, it feels like being a child again.

We work hard, and even though the house isn't really finished, as as soon as it is enclosed, we move in. When the bathtub gets plumbed we wash dishes in it. The kitchen is far from finished, so we cook in the trailer, or outside on our Weber BBQ. The first night in the house I say goodnight to the girls. Grace luxuriates in her own little bedroom. Mary Lea bursts into tears.

"What's wrong, don't you like your new bedroom?" I ask her.

"It's just that we are, well, we're so far away from each other," she says. She misses her trailer bunk bed. I realize for all of her six years, she's shared a very small room with her older sister. For at least four of those years, she's slept in a bunk-bed. This is a big change for her—for all of us.

In order to get our final inspection, we have to move the trailer off the land; the county insists. We rented the trailer to a guy who's handy. He was the same one who fixed our old white truck with my hair pin, before we really knew him. He also smokes like crazy and whenever he opened the trailer door a puff of hazy smoke swirled out. We feel both relieved and bad when we give him his notice. We put an ad in the local paper and a guy comes to look. He buys the trailer. The next day he's back to get it, and we sadly wave good bye to Hi

Ho Silver as it exits out the circular drive.

Grace has been given an old horse, Comet, and every morning he sticks his tawny head in the big opening where someday French doors will swing open onto a deck. The horse knows we'll give him an apple. We try to keep him away from the vegetable garden. We don't want him to founder, or the garden to disappear. We plan to eat from it over the summer. Grace and I have to go for bales of hay in the old truck. Our golden retriever barks at anything that comes near the place. From all outward appearances we're a happy and lucky family.

But the next year, Grace has a prophetic dream. She sees Comet dead in a pool of blood. She starts to call friends who have pastures or ranches to see if they can take Comet. I can't figure it out, she loves that horse, but she wants him off the land.

It's too late. She comes crying into the bedroom one morning, "I told you we had to move Comet and now he's out there dead. He's covered with blood. Oh Mom, it's terrible. I let him down."

I hug her and try my best to reassure her, but realize I should have paid closer attention. She has the dubious gift of second sight.

We call a company to come get the carcass. I tell Grace and Mary Lea to stay in the house and not to look out the windows. A dark man with curly hair, calm, sweet and reassuring says, "I'm sorry, I know this is hard for all of you." He uses a crane mounted on the truck to lift Comet into the back and then drives the truck out of the pasture. I go out to pay him as Grace and Mary Lea sob in Grace's room. He drives away taking Grace's beloved, and our funny friendly pet, off to the rendering plant. We didn't ask exactly what would become of the horse, but something to do with tallow, was printed on the side of his big rickety truck.

That was a very bad day for the whole family. Losing Comet was a bump and made us all feel that life was not going to be roses roses after all, out here in paradise.

One of our new neighbors, Bruce Bordi, who had turned our plans into blueprints for building permits heard about Comet and comes over to cheer us up. Bruce and Scott begin an impromptu concert. Bruce plays his accordion, and Scott a harmonica. We're surprised about the accordion, but he is Italian. Then, Bruce tells us he's related to old Emil Bordi who used to play at the Union Hotel.

"Emil!" I say, "Your cousin is part of what made me fall in love with Occidental!"

We laugh, and relax into the star sprinkled night.

We have started over. Scott and I talk of renewed commitment. Our lives will be better here; we will be better. We will make our own yogurt, keep our marriage vows, garden in the nude and look for a folk dancing class. We will find our way, without a compass, at the West Pole.

Driving Blind

Careening around corners, around blind curves,
driving west, driving blind.
Filled with hay bales,
kids in the back,
careening around corners,
driving west, driving blind.
Sun makes the white truck shine,
dust fogs the windshield.
Driving blind.

The White Truck: AKA Sleeping Beauty

One day my husband arrives driving a 1962 Ford pickup the color of dirty snowballs. "We need this," Scott says, "for all the stuff we'll be hauling. You know, hay for the horse, lumber, gravel, and building supplies."

He doesn't mention the obvious, that it's no beauty; it's big and bulky, rusty and dented. It's got no automatic transmission, no power steering, and from previous experience with old heaps, I know it's a gas hog. It will be my car, he explains. He'll commute to San Francisco in the VW bus.

I can handle it, I think. I've been raised on trucks. And I've just found out I'm pregnant. I've been walking to town, but it's two miles across neighbors' lands, and down curvy, narrow Bittner Road, and soon, I'll have a baby on my back. The truck, even if it's a rusted piece of junk, will make life easier.

Following a tradition of naming our funky old cars, we vote on a name for the truck. The girls' name wins and the truck is christened "Sleeping Beauty." Somehow it fits. It's just waiting for a kiss from a prince to change into a lovely Audi or perhaps a BMW, or even a new Toyota pickup.

As I learn to shift its peculiar gears, and, with no power steering, wrestle it around curves, deer, and fallen trees, I regularly lose loads. Gravel, hay, turkey manure and lumber fly into the dirt. Like a homing pigeon, the truck has a primal instinct for ditches. I just can't control it as it lunges into trouble. The men on our road find this amusing. They make a lot of woman driver jokes at my expense, and they do it so I'm sure to hear.

When Rowan, our new baby girl, is a few weeks old, I put her into her tote basket, decorated with ribbons by our new neighbors and friends, and slide it onto the passenger seat to take her down to the Occidental Area Health Center. It's time for her first well baby check-up.

I'm finally getting the hang of driving the white truck, even though Sleeping Beauty still has a mind of her own. Just when I begin to trust her, she betrays me. On my way down the hill into Occidental the truck's gas pedal falls uselessly to the floor. Like a bewildered man with a lost erection, the truck coasts to a stop. I'm getting the baby out when a guy in a little Toyota truck pulls up behind me and parks.

"Need help?"

"I can't believe it," I tell him, "The gas pedal just suddenly fell flat."

He's a brawny mechanically confident type.

"Probably lost the cotter pin."

"What?" I ask.

"Never mind," he says, hoisting up Sleeping Beauty's hood. "'Have any wire?"

I think for a minute, then dig a long thick hairpin from my unruly mass of hair. "Will this work?" I ask as I hand it to him.

"Perfect," he says, twisting the pin through a few holes and into some coupling for the gas pedal. His fingers are as fat as little British banger sausages, but skilled like those of a safe-cracker. Truck fixed, baby Rowan and I proceed to the Health Center.

When we arrive we're greeted by an angry receptionist.

"You're late," the receptionist scolds. Without the hair pin to secure it in place, my hair's a curly tumbled down mess: I don't really know how to explain why I'm late.

"I know, I'm so very sorry. I had some problems getting here."

A few weeks later I'm supposed to be driving the VW bus to Mill Valley to meet friends for lunch. I've arranged ahead of time with Scott to use the camper that day, but his plans change, so I end up driving Sleeping Beauty. When I arrive at the restaurant with Rowan in her basket, the driver's side door refuses to open more than a crack. I try nudging it with my shoulder and finally lean back and give it a good kick. It flings open. People outside the restaurant stop and stare as I carefully step down in my high heels and front-wrap dress. "A little mechanical difficulty," I say smiling.

"Are you Diane Keaton?" A woman on the sidewalk suddenly asks.

"What makes you think that?" I ask dumbfounded.

"You are her, aren't you!" she insists. I'm late and irritated, and I need to nurse the baby and use the ladies room. I point to the truck,

"Would Diane Keaton be driving this wreck?" I practically scream.

"Oh, I see what you mean," she says walking away as fast as she can.

My Mill Valley friends, who've seen it all through the window, think the whole truck thing's a hoot. They're laughing. They're the same ones who, for our going away party, had boxed up chickens, drugged them a little to keep them quiet, and wrapped the box in lovely paper with a big bow. We left the hens in Tam Valley with a friend, promising to return for the chickens when we built a coop, which never happened.

As I drive home from Mill Valley, Rowan asleep in her basket, I think about the woman mistaking me for Diane Keaton. I remember the movie *Annie Hall* with those lobsters crawling all over the place. What would Diane Keeton/Annie Hall do if she had to deal with power outages, loads of turkey manure, and a funky old truck, gas pedal held together with a woman's hairpin? She would probably just smile and climb back in the truck, and then time after time, drive into the nearest ditch.

The driver's side truck door refuses to open from the inside for most of the rest of the time I drive it.

Once I sit in the truck with a cute guy and kiss. Now, maybe I shouldn't tell on myself, but its part of a bigger story, the story of Sleeping Beauty.

When my husband is out of town as usual at his spiritual community, with his guru, I arrange for the kids to stay with neighbors and go off to meet a young man friend for dinner. We eat and drink a little and he gets more charming by the minute. We sit in my truck talking and kissing. He's upset. He tells me that his mother's just married, for the seventh time.

"I think she's a little crazy," he observes.

"Maybe she's always looking for something she can't find," I say. I feel the warmth of his hand on my thigh through my jeans. He's on his way to finding what he wants I think.

"I don't know why," he says, "but I'm really attracted to you." He kisses me again. "Do you think I look like Diane Keaton?" I ask.

"No," he says, "You remind me of that woman in the movie where she's carrying a painting across the street and the wind grabs the painting and ..."

"Jill Clayburgh—*An Unmarried Woman*," I say. "You've got to get out of the truck. I've got to go home." Somehow my being Jill Clayburgh is just too much to contemplate.

I turn the key. There's a series of clicks and nothing else. I try again. Nothing.

"Battery or ignition," he offers.

I climb into his car and drive to the nearest phone booth to call AAA. We awkwardly wait in his car for the tow truck.

"Why do you keep that old thing?" He finally asks.

"It's money and we need it for hay and stuff like that," I say, getting defensive.

"Shit," he says, "You should make your husband buy you a new one."

This guy doesn't understand anything, I think. I don't hear from him again, except once when he's drunk and calls to tell me his mother died.

A neighbor needs to borrow the truck. One of the guys who's teased me about the truck in the past is after a load of gravel.

"I don't need it back until this afternoon." I tell him. "Watch it, the truck pulls to the left."

When the truck isn't home by four o'clock, I walk down the road. There's the guy, truck stuck in a ditch. He's shoveling spilled gravel into a wheelbarrow.

"Tow truck's on the way," he says, not looking up. "It's really hard to control with all that gravel in the back," he offers. "It fishtails like crazy!" He doesn't really need to explain but I listen with a big grin on my face.

"Mind of her own," I add.

When I go to feed a neighbor's horses, our golden retriever tries to eat four of their chickens. I can't just leave them there badly mangled. I call around for help. "Could you just use an ax on their necks?" But no one can or will. I wipe away tears, close the half-dead chickens into a big cardboard box and take them to my driveway. I get the keys to the truck and use it to run the box over and over until I'm sure the birds are dead. I bury the box and call my neighbor at his law office in Santa Rosa. I grimace when he picks up the phone. I tell him my dog has killed his hens and offer to buy replacements.

"What happened, did the dog eat them?" he asks.

"Truthfully," I pause, "they were a mess, and I had to run them over with the white truck to put them out of their misery." First there's silence and then the lawyer, says, "With Sleeping Beauty?" He bursts out laughing and doesn't stop. I hang up the phone and go take a walk. Another country legend is born.

We're always broke, and to save a little money, we don't register the truck. Since we rarely take it out of Occidental, we're not worried. But one day, I need to take the girls into Sebastopol and promptly get a ticket for no current registration. I forget about it until two sheriff's deputies, guns drawn appear at my little shop in Occidental where I sit breast feeding Rowan. "So," I say, "You're going to take my baby and me to jail? And for what?"

"Oh, we're taking your baby to the dependents unit," they say, "and you to jail for failure to pay your registration on a 1962 Ford truck."

"Wow," I say, getting a little testy, "you guys must really be hard up to pull your guns on a mother who hasn't paid her truck registration. My neighbor's a lawyer and I'm calling him right now!"

"Where's the truck? It wasn't at your place," they say.

I worry that maybe they've seen the three pot plants growing out in half-barrels on the new deck, but they say nothing; it's the truck they're after.

"Stuck in the mud out in the horse pasture," I say.

"Okay, just pay the registration and we'll let you go. Or send in the registration saying the truck's abandoned." They re-holster their guns and walk away.

I'm not abandoning the truck—not yet. I'm still giving Sleeping Beauty her chance to wake up and prove that she's really a princess.

A couple of months later we get the new registration, so I feel it's safe to drive the truck to McNear's Brick Factory in San Rafael to pick through brick rejects to find only slightly damaged bricks at a penny a piece. I plan to get enough for a small brick patio in the front of the house where water always pools up creating a mud pit.

I'm wearing tattered jeans, my well worn Santa Rosa

construction boots, a long-sleeved, hooded red tee shirt and my work gloves. I love the clatter of the bricks as they bounce into the truck bed. I fill the bed and pay. It hardly costs anything. I'm proud of myself for getting these penny bricks. As I drive away, I see the truck's on empty so I head for a gas station. Suddenly there's the thumping of a tire going flat. "Damn!" I say, limping into the station. As I stand out in front to wait for my special saint—the AAA tow truck—a little grey Porsche drives up next to me. "Get in," says the driver. I'm not really listening. I'm distracted by a memory of my old red Porsche and how in 1965 I sold it because I was too pregnant with Grace to fit behind the steering wheel.

"Get in!" he insists. "Here," he pats the passenger seat of his sports car. Now he's got my full attention. I'm in the seedy part of town. He thinks I'm one of those car prostitutes!

"Jesus Christ," I say, "that's my truck over there with the flat. I'm waiting for a tow truck. Jesus," I mutter again.

"Oh shit," he says, screeching off. Probably thinks I might kick his ass. Trucks change a man's perception of a woman. I look down at myself covered in brick dust, and laugh until finally I'm crying by the time the tow truck arrives.

"I know you're upset, but this is the last time this year you can use your card. You've had too many calls," the AAA driver explains.

"I'm sorry," he says patting me on the shoulder. He leans down to jack up the truck. He sweats and struggles. With all those brick rejects in the truck bed, Sleeping Beauty is heavy. "Don't worry though, in four months you'll have your new card," he assures me pulling off the flat tire.

"It's okay," I stammer, "it's really okay." With a new tire on, I proceed to carefully and slowly drive the load of bricks home. Beauty and I successfully avoid all ditches.

I take a weekend hostess job at a winery. The owner likes to talk about grape harvesting, his favorite old movies, and since he knows I'm a tapper, he tells me about times when he was a tap dancer in New York City. One day, though, when he sees me arrive and kick my way out of the truck, his mouth forms the letter "O," and he turns away. Now he's categorized me. I'm among the unwashed. And literally that's true when I'm late to work because of the truck's failure to start, or because it's been stuck in the mud. I learn to park the truck up at the top of the property with a bale of hay in the back for balance, and bring a change of clothing. Mud-spattered jeans and boots are not what wine connoisseurs expect. But on a mucky boots day, a taster asks

"Are you related to the Fondas?"

"Gee, no," I say, "I'm related to Diane Keaton."

The final straw with Sleeping Beauty is when the girls tell me that Scott lets them take turns steering the truck down Coleman Valley Road, just about the most narrow and twisty road in the county. Mary Lea loves it, but says that sometimes Rowan gets scared and cries. Careening around corners, with tires squealing and Beauty lurching all over the road, I can't blame a toddler, or anyone, for that matter, for feeling afraid! Once again, Scott proves his need for adventure and breaking the rules. We get into a big fight about it, and I finally decide it's time for Sleeping Beauty to find a new home.

"I swear," I say, "We're getting rid of that truck. We can pick up hay in a station wagon. Our building project's over."

Scott mutters that a building project is never over. Miraculously, when another country bumpkin comes to look at the truck, the door works, and the gas pedal seems permanently fixed with the hair pin. He buys the truck. A new prince has Sleeping Beauty. Maybe he'll be the one to awaken her to her true sweetness.

The Tap Dancing Birthday Cake

What were they thinking? The cake costume, an ingenious, lovely construction of wooden bars and wire covered in white satin, has no armholes. Like ballast, arms are necessary to keep the tap dancer going, generate energy, and balance the legs with the rest of the body.

It's not just the lack of arms, which means less of a dance, but I can't shake hands, hold a drink, or even wave goodbye. The shape of the costume itself is limiting. Like a belly in the last months of pregnancy, the cake's in the way. There will be no hugging, no leaning into a good looking man, and no potty breaks.

Tonight I'm doing my second gig as *The Tap Dancing Birthday Cake*. It's a step above jumping out of a cake. The mixed message of humor with a lot of leg in fish net stockings intrigues the customers. This new job came with the new house, new schools and new car pool. Even with all this newness, I'm returning to the old place, Marin County, for this job. That's where people have the money to pay for a singing, or in this case, a tap dancing, greeting card, just for the hell of it.

I've navigated two sets of stairs and knocked, tapped really, on the door with my shoe, the front tap making a loud clatter that immediately brings the hostess to the door. She's wearing a sexy black negligee. When I look around the room, everyone is in some sort of sleeping attire. She sees the look on my face and says, "It's a slumber party."

Now the music starts. *"Will you still need me, will you still feed me, when I m 64?"* the Beatles ask. The insecurity of relationships and aging. I over-exaggerate the steps to draw attention away from the lack of arm action as I clinch my teeth into a great big smile because, if nothing else, a dancing cake who is only 37 years old should be happy.

A man calls out, "Beautiful!" I don't know if he means the dancing or me, but it keeps me tapping. A small droplet of perspiration clings to my chin just below the place where the strap from the cone-shaped hat digs into skin at the juncture of cheek and jaw. Now I've come to the part of "trenches" where arms, if I could use them, would swing rapidly back and forth along with the legs. Instead, my arms lie trapped beneath frothy fabric icing, squished below the shoulder mechanism that holds the costume together. Still, my legs fly, making satisfying scrapes against the plywood. Inadvertently arm and finger muscles twitch inside the cake. Out of habit they want to be part of the act.

My new friend, Sara, describes this job as "a perverse form of therapy." I'm working my way back to being the fast-paced mother-worker-bee. The cake is part of the plan. If I can be the cake, then it will all work out somehow.

I haven't told my husband about the underpants, satin to match the cake, with the words "Happy Birthday" written on the backside. His response to the new job has been, "When are you going to get over it? Now you're just making a spectacle of yourself!"

The panties, my little secret, stretching tightly across my rear. Intended to get a laugh, or something else.

It's not necessarily sexy being a tap dancing birthday cake. The job just doesn't feel right and I know I've got to quit, but just when I don't know. The question whirls through my mind in time to the music. The binding discomfort of the costume feels familiar, like a swaddling cloth meant to keep the baby from crying.

I almost trip just now on the "maxi ford," *jump shuffle jump*, probably too much for the plywood platform's uneven surface. The plywood, delivered with the music earlier in the day, a surprise for the two birthday boys' 40th. One of their wives has told me that they were fraternity brothers at Stanford.

Finally the sweat droplet falls from my chin, leaving a small round mark as it soaks into the wood. Claustrophobia is only a few tap steps away. The golden rosettes bounce around as I dance. This cake is about to slide off its platter onto the ground and ruin a good party.

The music concludes, and I turn away and tip the cake to get the Happy Birthday laugh and titillate the easy marks. Then I bow. I want it sort of balletic, except that without arms extended, I simply wobble. For a minute, the room spins in a haze of color. This is the time that's hardest, when people expect the cake to stick around and join the party. Be good for a few more laughs. Fear lights up my eyes, but the crowd probably sees it as excitement, the two emotions like fraternal twins.

"Fantastic legs," one of the birthday boys says, lips curling back to expose a perfect set of white teeth. Probably an orthodontist. "Can I get you a drink? Oh, no, I guess unless I pour the drink down your throat... there's no way for you to drink, is there?"

"Thanks anyway," I say through clenched teeth, "Oh yes, and Happy Birthday!"

A short, rotund man spews bits of alcohol-laden saliva into my face as he says, "You know, I can get you a job that will make you some <u>real</u> money!" If I had a hand, I would slap him, but I simply pull a cake-like u-turn and walk toward the door, my face red and sweaty.

The hostess comes over with an envelope of money for the talent agency. "Oh, dear, well, I guess I'll just tuck this under your hat," she says, pulling the already strained rubber chin-strap aside and sticking the envelope up into the cone, wriggling the silver mylar flames that are affixed to the top of the hat. My curly hair, unleashed for a minute, springs out from under the cone.

"Thanks," I mutter, as the strap snaps back into its comfortable fleshy niche. "You were great, everyone loved you. Can't you stay a little longer?" coos the co-hostess.

"Got to get home," I say. "I'm glad it all worked out," I add, no real personality coming through. Just trying to maintain before I scream. At least I can run and scream, if I need to. No arms required. She opens the door for me, bell shaped cake knocking against the door frame.

The stairs are misted by fog. I take a deep breath. My heart pounds and for a minute I stand frozen at the top. The thought of going back into a mob of drunken party-goers seems even scarier, so I Ginger Rogerly take that first step down, aware that taps can be very slippery. On the second step, I curse the lack of arms again.

It would be easy to fall to the bottom, creating a fatal head injury and ripping the cake costume into tiny, shiny shards. The girls would cry and my husband might miss me, might have regrets about his fondness for moms in the car pool. I think of a perfectly round little yellow pill with a heart shaped cutout in the center, a *Mother's Little Helper*, but there is none of that now.

As I reach the landing at the bottom of the stairs, I let out the breath I'd been holding and take in another, cold air stinging a little. Maybe disappearing isn't such a bad idea. I could fling myself down, falling and tumbling, rolling like an unexploded stick of dynamite down the hilly streets. Arms pinned to my sides, panties bumping against cement, wire twisting free. Gaining momentum, I'd disappear, never to be seen or heard from again. A blur of white, scattering a trail of tattered rosettes, hat a madly whirling glow of silver and neon pink against the darkness.

In the cool night air by my car I practically stand on my head, and hoist up the shoulder mechanism to get the cake off. Yoga helps. Then I let it fall to the ground, collapse the thing and fit it into the back of my VW camper. I take off the black patent tap shoes and put on my furry slippers and a pair of warm, comfortable sweat pants and sweatshirt.

I'm on my way heading back to home sweet home. When I cross the Marin/Sonoma County line driving home, I tell myself I don't really want or need this gig as the Tap Dancing Birthday Cake anymore. I'm going to call the company and tell them, "This cake quits!"

The money's good, but the gigs are stressful. I thought it might get me past a few things. Get me over the lack of a husband's attentions. But it just makes me more of a fool than I already am. Put that Joker away, put the Fools card back in the Tarot deck and move on, I tell myself as I accelerate down 101.

After an hour's drive I pull into our driveway. There's no fog—just dark tree silhouettes, a deeply starry sky, and the crunch of gravel against the tires.

Critters List

Things to look out for around here:

Widow makers: branches that detach and hang high up in a tree; they fall later.

Black widow spiders: look for a red violin on a fat black body.

Hobo spiders: related to brown recluses; nasty habit of laying eggs in a wound.

Ticks and Lyme disease: little ticks fill with blood, transfer the disease from deer.

Scorpions: nasty stinger.

Rattlesnakes: diamonds on back, rattles a warning; don't go near.

Coyotes: howl, yip, eat rodents and small household pets; keep pets inside.

Foxes: tails streak out behind as they run; can carry rabies.

Mountain lions: scream, yell, prowl a large terrain; they eat deer, sometimes pets.

Sea lions: when calving, stay back.

Raccoons: fierce; raid houses for food; come in cat doors; fight with dogs.

Big owls: beautiful night creatures sometimes known to carry away cats.

Ferrets: related to weasels and badgers; mean-tempered, not
   often seen.
Badgers: beautiful, but make excavations that can wreck the
   terrain.
Black bears: cinnamon-colored; love berries and compost piles.
Gophers: gobble up gardens; these ground rats drove the
   Russians out.
Blackberry and wild raspberry: watch the brambles, they can
   scratch and sting.
Poison oak: three leaves; don't touch; swelling, itching,
   burning.
Floods: mostly on roads during heavy downpours and
   occasionally the Russian River.
Leaning fir trees: small root systems; the tall tree most likely
   to tumble over.
Blind curves: winding roads, drive with care.
Curvaceous women: look out, danger ahead.

Not for Wimps

My mother and I pick blackberries along the side of the road, our fingers stained purple. Blackberries are still a new delight.

"Seems like a good spot for black bear," she says dropping another handful of berries into our bucket.

"I hope not," I say to her laughing. "There are plenty of other scary critters. Sometimes we hear mountain lions screaming in the dead of night."

"Do they roar, or growl?" she asks.

"Sounds like a woman screaming for help," I say. "Makes the hair on my arms stand up."

I'm a Southern Californian and my husband Scott is from Chicago. Worlds apart in every way. We're struggling to salvage our marriage just as we've salvaged wood, clawfooted tubs and old windows for the house we're building. We aren't prepared for the rough and tumble life of country dwelling, but we share a love of nature. Somehow moving here to the country, surrounded by beauty and staying very busy with property care and house building and kids seems like a good idea.

It's 1979 and we've lived here in the country for two years. Recently a tree, a "twin" with two tops, split apart, shattering across our new rock driveway. We heard it come crashing down. We imagine it is the first of many times we'll hear the trees fall in the forest. The sound of two hands clapping.

Scott got out the chain saw and set to work cutting off branches and cutting up the tree trunk into pieces small enough to carry off the drive. Our young daughters stood around watching this version of their tall, wiry, dad, (whom they usually see running 14-mile half-marathons). After a while they got bored and went back inside the house to play Old Maid and Crazy Eights. I know I will never have the courage to pick up a chain saw and use it, unless I have to. I've heard that people around here carry chain saws in the backs of their trucks, in the trunks of their cars.

Scott is often in San Francisco. He hasn't yet transfered his work up here. It feels like I'm on my own a lot and anything challenging seems to happen when he's gone.

One November afternoon, our golden retriever barks like crazy. I go out into the rain to find a big red fox, about the size of our retriever, violently shaking in the middle of our drive.

I hurry back in the house. "What the hell is wrong with the thing?" I say out loud as I pick up the phone to call the closest neighbor.

"What hell, Mom, what?" Grace, the older daughter asks. As I describe the animal's behavior, both girls run out to see the fox before I have time to stop them.

"Rabies," my neighbor Bruce says, "I'll be right over."

I rush out to grab the girls and the retriever. I shut the door and explain:

"There's going to be a loud noise. It'll be Bruce shooting that fox because it's sick and there's nothing we can do to help it."

The girls protest and cry and cover their ears so they won't hear the rifle go off. Afterwards Bruce knocks on the door.

"You'll have to call the county to come get the carcass. This rabid fox will become a part of some type of collected data."

"Thanks," I say.

As Bruce turns to leave, our striped tabby cats amble out of the woods.

"Watch your cats at night," Bruce says, "the owls around here carry them off."

At this moment, I realize that life in the country isn't for wimps. And I am one, and here I am with two kids, and as I've just discovered, a third one on the way.

When I go into labor with our youngest daughter in 1980, the house is mostly finished. Things are fairly comfortable for us now. I lie in bed while a plumber does the last hook up for the bathroom sink. I wait as long as I can before I call Scott to say I need to go to the hospital. He's at a neighbor's watching a golf tournament on TV. Our TV isn't working yet.

It's dark when we head for Santa Rosa in a big rainstorm. Areas of Graton Road are covered with water. Atascadero Creek has jumped its banks. Scott eases the Volkswagen camper into the water, even though volunteer firemen in their yellow and red slickers with red fire hats flag him down and yell for him to stop. I'm lying in the back clutching my belly and moaning.

"Turn back, buddy, turn it around. Nobody comes through here," the volunteer firefighter orders him.

"Sorry, man, wife's in labor, got to get to the hospital."

"Well, okay, buddy, good luck," the volunteer fireman says. "Take it slow and easy when you get to the Laguna de Santa Rosa; the bridge is close to flooded."

After forty minutes we're at the hospital, but a few hours later labor stops and we are sent back home, crossing the same flooded places again. Two days later I'm in hard labor and my husband calls Dr Rosa. He will meet us at the Occidental Area Health Center. Grace is 14, and Mary Lea 9, and we wake them up to say the baby is going to be born. "Mom, that's what you've said before a few times," Grace says. "We'll just stay here and sleep," She turns back over and pulls the quilt over her head

When we get down the hill, Dr. Rosa looks me over on an examining table and says, "You're not leaving here. It's going to be very soon now. " And sure enough a third daughter is delivered on that very same examining table, one of a handful of babies delivered in our rural health center.

It's a small-town birth. The doctor, his wife, and the nurse called in to help, are all friends now. We play volleyball and drink beer together. When we leave the center, it's 5:30 in the morning. Scott bangs on the kitchen door of LandHouse Bakery and the bakers come out to see the baby and bring Cheese Danish for us. When we get home we show the baby to her sleepy sisters. "Cute," they say in unison. "But Mom, she looks a little like that cartoon character, Mr. Magoo," Mary Lea adds.

All the names we've picked don't fit, or the older girls reject. This baby is from generations of redheads. Her heritage includes Scots, Welsh, Irish, Dutch and Native American. They are hardy people and tall. We decide on the name Rowan. It's means tree and red. She's an adventurous sort. As a toddler, before I realize she's gone, neighbors call to say she's at their house a half mile down the road. Later she travels the world and marries someone from Africa. She can deal with life in the country, it turns out.

In 1981, the biggest of several floods on the nearby Russian River makes the news. It's in the paper and on TV.

"Let's go see it," Scott says. "

He's a thrill seeker. He'd love to cross a few streams, and drive the car under half-downed trees and bring his Nikon camera to record it all.

"We'll take the girls and give them an education. They're old enough for it," he adds.

The baby is a year old and the other girls now are 10 and 15.

"Don't worry, worry wart, the Volkswagen camper is made for this, we can get there. Remember last year when you were in labor," Scott says.

"What worries me," I say, "is that you're making this an adventure when it could be a disaster. "

"Oh, come on," he says.

"Yeah, we want to see the flood," Mary Lea says.

"We do, Mom," says her sister Grace. They're cut from the same cloth.

In the end I don't want to seem like a wimp, so I go along. I pack up the kids, bring blankets, water, a flashlight, and diapers for the baby, just in case we get stranded somewhere. I pack a basket with cups and plates, some sandwiches and bananas and juice. It feels a little like a disaster picnic. Scott hands me his ever handy flask of vodka, just in case we might need it. "For medicinal purposes." He looks at me and shrugs. I hand it back and he tucks it into his jacket pocket.

We drive north for twenty minutes on the winding Bohemian Highway alongside raging Dutch Bill Creek, white foam everywhere, and the water as close to the road as I've ever seen it. We find a spot above the flood zone, up a hill with a good view of the Monte Rio bridge, which is totally covered by the flood waters. I'm horrified to see propane tanks hurtling by, small homes and other detritus tossing, churning, and roiling down the muddy flood waters of the Russian River and out to sea. We even hear a propane tank blow up as it bounces against the trees and rocks along the riverbanks.

"Jeez," Scott says.

"Wow," say the two older girls.

"Did you see that house, a whole house, in the river!" Mary Lea asks.

"Mama! Mama!" the little one says, pointing, copying her sisters. She can't really talk yet, but she too feels it; it's powerful. Then without saying anything more, Rowan curls back into her nest of blankets and goes to sleep. The same technique she uses years later when, in my next marriage, we all go to family therapy together.

"Mom, now I understand your fear," my oldest daughter says.

She gets it, the reach of the muddy waters, the raw destruction of it, the uprooted trees tumbling headfirst in the river. Boats and docks and people's furniture and cars submerged.

It's a real scene. Scott wanders away from the car in the rain clicking pictures, taking a few sips from his flask as he goes.

"Oh this makes me feel awful, everything people are losing," I say to him when he comes back to the car. I begin to cry. "Let's go home now."

To me, a flood isn't a spectator sport, and I don't want to encourage adrenaline rushes in my children. Let them get it later on from skiing or surfing or reading a thrilling book, or maybe from that first boyfriend.

On the drive home everyone in the car is quiet. But then Scott says, "That was just amazing! Just f-ing amazing! I think I got some great pictures."

I start to understand that most action photographers and maybe even the famous fashion photographers, the paparazzi, are all voyeurs.

High winds howl all night long, whistling through the cracks at the bottom of the French doors and sending branches crashing and flying through the air. On our battery-powered radio, we hear that it's an 80-mile-an hour wind, practically hurricane force, and roads are closed and power out for miles around. We have a propane stove and wood heat and gravity-feed water from the well, so we're basically all right. But a few days ago, even before this storm, our power went off when a redwood tree's waterlogged roots gave way and the tree crashed across the power lines leading to the west county. Now what we suffer from is cabin fever.

Mary Lea is 13 and wants to do some holiday shopping in Santa Rosa.

She's her father's daughter: Some fun might come of it. As usual, I cave in to the more persistent voice and we head out. At least the wind has stopped, and rain no longer pounds down in thick sheets, turning the roads into streams.

"Let's turn back," I say as we come across yet another obstacle, having to find a third choice route into town. Trees, mudslides, and downed power lines are everywhere.

"Mom, you're always ready to quit! Where's your sense of adventure?"

Once in Hawaii it took me half an hour to let go and slide down the chute over a waterfall into a deep pool below. When my head bobbed up in the water, I was greeted by a round of applause. *Maybe she's right,* I think. *Maybe it'll be fine.*

Mary Lea continues her pitch: "I'm feeling crazy from being inside all the time. I haven't done any shopping for Christmas. And I'd like to hear some music. You don't understand, Mom, how hard it is for me not to listen to Michael Jackson!"

This is in the days before iPods and iPhones and iTunes. The olden days.

"Like Dad says, don't be such a wimp!" She's adds this with a thrust of a saber. These kids know how to work me.

On our third detour attempt we come across volunteer firemen. They're cutting up a huge downed fir tree and pulling it to the side of the road. They're neighbors and friends, and mostly young and mostly men with a sense of mission. They are the first to accidents, fires and emergencies of any kind. Without pay.

"Hey, hi, what do you think, can we get through to Santa Rosa?" I ask.

"I don't know, it's pretty bad out there," Mike Gonella says. His family owns the Union Hotel restaurant in town. "More trees might come down. The ground's saturated and their roots got a good work out from the wind. A redwood came down this morning on a house and the woman reading on her couch was trapped under heavy limbs and ceiling material. I'm afraid she may have a broken spine."

"Oh crap," I say, "that sounds bad! Anyway, just want to say thanks for being our heroes."

"Someone's got to do it," he says smiling, moving aside the yellow hazard tape to let us through. "Be careful," he says.

Eventually we make our way to the shopping mall where all is warm and bright, cheerful and cozy. The colorful Christmas lights practically blind us after so many days of living by candlelight and a Coleman lantern. It jars me, the contrast between what we've seen and been through to get here, and the Christmas jingles and holy music and people tossing coins and dollars into Salvation Army boxes as the ever present jangling bells ring. Mary Lea finds a few *Hello Kitty* things for Rowan and some inexpensive jewelry for Grace and some cute socks for friends. She's beaming as she drinks her hot chocolate at the food bar.

"Isn't it worth it? Aren't you glad we came?" she asks

"Hmm, sure," I say, finishing up my cocoa. I don't feel like revealing my troubled state of mind—how I'm thinking again about the woman who may have a broken spine, wondering if it's someone I know. Already I'm dreading the drive home.

By the time we get home, miraculously, after five days without, we have power! Christmas lights of our own are twinkling, and music, old Renaissance Christmas tunes played on baroque instruments, blares from the living room stereo.

"Twee, Mama, twee" Rowan says, delighted. She is seeing her first Christmas lights ever, put up by her dad and oldest sister while we're in Santa Rosa.

"Lights, colorful Christmas lights on the tree," I reply. I've never been much for baby talk.

It's 1982 and I'm hiking a dirt road, cutting over to the main road to town from our place. I have a fabric store, and it's about a two mile walk in. I often take this short cut. Like in an old Tintoretto painting, sunshine filters through dark tree branches onto abundant green. It's dramatic and ominously gorgeous. I hear something nearby snort. I stop, listen, and look around. A huge buck deer with a full rack of antlers stands in the forest just to the side of me. He looks at me and I stare back for a full minute. I admire his shaggy scar-pocked fur and his large, confident stance. I'm tempted to bolt, but something deep inside me says to hold my ground. The buck breathes heavily and keeps looking at me. He's at least a foot taller than I am and probably a hundred or more pounds heavier. He's majestic and scary. Suddenly, he turns away and crashes

off into the brush and up the hill. I shake and smile and talk to myself all at the same time. "Did I really see what I thought I saw?" A refrain that becomes my country mantra.

We're close to the Pacific Ocean. Storms roll in, their moisture grabbed by redwoods and firs. These trees love water and drink gallons and gallons of it. Cazadero, just north of us, gets 85 inches of rain a year. The second wettest town in

California, it's fecund, and damp, with mold spores just awaiting that first sunny day to burst out.

The trees are magnets for lightning strikes. I've seen smoldering trees split in half along the sides of Jonive and Occidental Roads. Even at Osmosis, the spa down the hill, a lightning strike blew apart an oriental-styled structure with a metal spire. It sat in the middle of the meditation pond with Buddha sitting next to it as a witness to the blast. The noise is phenomenal. Nature at full force.

"I love these thunderstorms, they're so energizing, so exciting," my neighbor who grew up in the Midwest tells me.

I don't tell her that they terrify me and my dog. Thunder usually sends me crashing to the floor in a fetal position.

We listen to thunderclaps rumble across the ridge, going south, down towards Tomales Bay and Pt. Reyes Station, getting fainter and fainter. I feel relief until the next wave of thunder sends me and my dog back to the floor.

In late February, I enjoy driving during a break in the rainstorms. It's lambing season in Petaluma, and on the back roads, flocks of mother sheep with their babies graze in pastures. As I round a bend on the Valley Ford-Two Rock Road I see a sheep, fluffy white against verdant green leap up awkwardly, again and again, at a vulture whose wingspan is almost as wide as her whole body. Finally the vulture ascends. I chuckle at how funny it looks, almost like out of a cartoon. But, then, I'm gripped by a dark reality; this is a mother defending her lamb, her dead baby which she doesn't accept as dead yet. My whole focus shifts. Just like life in the country, it's real, it's close, and not for the faint of heart. It's not, I remind myself, a place for wimps.

Fish Net Dreams

Women push
through tangled nets
over stars and men
through rose thickets
past magpie nests.

Thin fish net
curtains blow
on the breeze
over a mother
and her daughters
sleeping
by the window.

A full moon floods
through casements
lets in all light, all dreams
keeps out starfish,
and men with keys
shaped like fish,

dissolves entanglements
thread by thread.

Sewphie's: The Threads That
Bind Us Together

I have a love-hate relationship with my sewing machine. When it works well, I hum along, seams going down, something fun coming out the other side of the needle. When it's not going well, the thread balls up and I have to patiently untangle it, or wind more thread on a bobbin, or maybe, if the tension is too tight and breaks the thread, I have to slowly re-thread the whole thing. Sometimes I swear a lot. It's like life itself.

When I lived in Mill Valley, I was spoiled by a great store, Good Measure Fabrics. They carried unusual buttons, Vogue patterns, a line of chintz upholstery fabrics, oriental silks, threads and all the usual accoutrements of a sewing woman's paradise. But when I moved to Occidental in 1977, there just weren't any good fabric stores in Sonoma County. So in 1979 I decided to open one of my own.

I'd been working two part time jobs and didn't like either one. I also had an occasional third job working for a Marin County singing telegram company as a tap dancing birthday cake. I gave tap lessons to kids after school and taught an exercise class. I was finishing up the building of a house and raising kids. I needed the extra income for things like Grace's soccer uniforms and cheer-leading outfits and Mary Lea's music lessons, piano and voice. She's got a gift and I want to help her hone her musical skills.

At a party, I complain about all my different jobs, none of which I like.

"Ah come on, you know you love to work," Scott chimes in.

"I do like working, but I need to do one job, and one that means something to me, one that brings me joy," I say.

"Like what?" Scott asks.

"Well, I'm not sure, but I'd like to own a shop."

"Dream on," Scott says. The exchange, so public, is a little embarrassing, but I tuck the idea into my Fool's brain and work on it. I decide on a combination fabric and gift shop in downtown Occidental. I'm going to become a shopkeeper.

The town is home to a hip base of do-it-yourselfers, and a continuous supply of bored tourists looking for something to buy. But, as Scott points out, I have no real retail experience, know nothing much about business, about how to display merchandise, or how to promote a business. After being a contractor on our home, I feel more confident and I'm eager to tackle a new challenge. What could go wrong?

"Where in heck will you get the money for it?" Scott asks

"I can borrow from that real estate guy down the hill who lends."

"You mean take out a second on our house?" he says in disbelief.

"Well, since no one else is coming up with the money, it seems reasonable."

"Oh, crap, just go ahead, I know you'll do it anyway," he says, resigned to the fact.

I start the process for a small second mortgage loan and look around for a business partner.

I find a like-minded woman who sews and has chutzpah and she and I plan for four months. We check out other fabric stores in San Francisco, Berkeley, Palo Alto, and Mill Valley. We take notes, and we envision what we want in our store. We look at spaces available in downtown Occidental; there aren't many to choose from. We pick a name: *Sewphie's Country Dry Goods.*

From our own milled redwood trees—the ones we had to fell for our building site, lumber goes to a hunky blond carpenter who turns it into shelving and a big, smooth, redwood cutting table. We order greeting cards, Mrs. Grossman stickers, Chinese tai chi shoes, totes, and decorative pillows. We discover a local pattern company, Folkwear, and order a selection. The patterns have the most beautiful illustrations, little works of art all on their own. I learn as much about geography from the patterns as about sewing. There are Afghan Nomad dresses, Gaza dresses, Egyptian shirts, Syrian dresses, Turkish coats, Kimonos and Tibetan panel coats. I re-visit history, Missouri River Boatman's shirts, Prairie Dresses, Rodeo Cowgirl shirts, Victorian wear and children's patterns with kitschy names, like Little Kittels and Little Folks.

We order Tibetan felt boots, stitched in bright colors, with multi-colored layered soles. Locals bring in their wares—Salli Rasberry sells her hand-knit caps; Terri Jo, her tiny hand-dyed cotton baby clothes made on an old foot-powered treadle machine on the Wheeler Ranch. Regina brings in felt baby shoes with tiny roses on the toes of the girls' shoes and another seamstress, Monika, takes our Hawaiian fabrics and makes men's shirts for sale. It'll be a hippie's paradise at Sewphie's. Former commune dwellers and artful sewing ladies will line up for these fabrics, patterns, and gifts. Perhaps even a gent or two will wander into the store.

On the day we're to open our business account, I carefully tuck the realtor's check from the second mortgage into my purse. It's not much, but I think it's enough. I meet my future partner at the bank in Sebastopol. I'm happy, excited full of hope.

My partner-to-be breaks down crying when the teller explains that she cannot withdraw money from the joint account she has with her husband, because there is no money to withdraw.

"Oh my god, my husband has emptied that account," she says crying. "He didn't want me to do this, but he never told me he was taking all the money out! I'm so sorry but I guess I can't pursue my dream with you." She cries even harder and then, suddenly, turns and runs out the door. I don't hear from her, so I finally call. She confirms that she is out as my business partner.

I'm shaken but determined, so I put my money into a new business account and figure that I'll just have to find someone else.

I call the fabric salesman, who happens to live in Occidental, to tell him of my dilemma and he suggests his sister-in-law Susie might be interested.

"She's just back from the West Indies and is looking for something to get into. She's smart; she went to Stanford. And like you, she's got little kids," he says.

I ask all my new friends about her. She tells me later that she's done the same to find out about me. We pass the friends test, so we meet and talk. She's petite with long, pretty hair and a certain energetic glow. We like one another and begin what is to become a short business partnership but a long friendship. She agrees to do the bookkeeping and I will promote the business. We both will select merchandise and take turns running the store. We will try to accommodate each other's kids' schedules, and the kids can be in the store. It's not far for them to walk here after school.

On a whim, and out of a need to create something artsy for the store, I get out my jig saw and take some left-over construction plywood and cut out two mannequins. I drill holes to joint the arms, and wire them carefully together so the arms can be out straight, or hand-on-hip. Then I paint hair and faces onto the wood. One mannequin is a woman, one a child, probably a girl, but could be a boy. I struggle to get the blouse and dress on the dummies, but realize I'm the dummy who made these ridiculously impractical mannequins. I manage to get the clothes on them without bursting any seams and then stand the mannequins up in our display window. They look like giant paper dolls on a bad trip.

With help from our husbands, we hang up a cute chicken sign, the chicken standing for country stuff, nesting stuff. Like the Little Red Hen.

We take all the fabric that's been delivered and stack it onto the shelves, sorting by type of material and color. We stand back and admire our handiwork. Susie and I hug. I can hardly wait to get home and phone my mom and chat about it. I know she'll be excited for me. If Mom feels better, she and Dad may drive up for the store's opening. Mom's had cancer for so many years. Sometimes she's feeling pretty good, but sometimes she's feeling pretty bad. Recently she's undergone another round of chemotherapy. She'll rebound. She's a phoenix.

Scott brings the girls by and I think they're all impressed. It's real and it's pretty and it's here. They all seem happy, too. Blonde Grace and dark curly-haired Mary Lea each help themselves to a few stickers, and, for some reason, thread; I don't know why they want the thread.

"I like Sewphie's, Mom," Grace says pocketing another spool of thread. I can't help noticing how lanky she's getting. A pre-teen. "Me too," Mary Lea says cutting off another length of stickers. I puff up with a certain rooster-like pride, knowing that really I'm more of a little red hen.

We advertise our St. Patrick's Day opening and secretly hope for the luck of the Irish, even though they weren't always lucky. We want to make a splash, so we rent a furry white chicken costume, our mascot being a chicken. Two rather large women volunteer to take turns being the chicken and walk around town handing out flyers for Sewphie's. It's a hot day and the chickens sweat.

We attract a mob who wants to see what's new in little Occidental with its two-block-long main drag. We sell needle packets, thread, some cards and a few patterns, and give out a lot of little chicken stickers to kids. An older woman named Alice, who always comes to the library next door, shows us how to fill out a sales slip and figure the sales tax on our little hand calculator. We feel kind of foolish.

Later in the week, a tall stylish woman comes in and looks around and then goes outside and stares into the front window. This makes me uneasy, but maybe she is admiring our window display?

"I know this might sound funny, but I'd like to buy your mannequins."

I'm astounded.

"The mannequins in the window?"

"Yes, the mannequins, the only mannequins. How much do you want for them? Would you take one hundred dollars?" She is wearing a very chic pair of jeans with an expensive blue designer sweater and high heels. Not from around here, I think.

"Ummmmmm, let me think for a minute." My mind whirls. I think, what? Are you crazy! Finally I sputter, "Well, errrr, sure!"

I'm reminded of a time in Mill Valley when someone from a Sausalito art gallery came and bought all the completely goofy pillows I made for a co-op nursery school fundraiser. Even now, after continuing to show art in that gallery, and at many other venues, I still haven't fully accepted myself as an artist.

So our biggest sale of the week is the handmade wooden mannequins. I have to laugh later at the irony of having nowhere to hang the woman's Folkwear Gibson Girl blouse and a small Folkwear child's dress with pinafore I had made specially to go on the mannequins.

As it turns out, my new partner Susie, doesn't really know how to sew. She blurts it out a few weeks after we open the store. But she loves fabric. And like me, she loves the idea of being a shopkeeper. She doesn't mind that the shop looks very ordered from the front, but behind the counter lies chaos. We store our big bulky rolls of quilt batting in the bathtub next door, and tuck anything else that won't fit into the shop into empty corners. We're both okay with a certain amount of hidden disarray.

My dad calls to say they can't make it up for another month, but he wants to tell me what he thinks of my new business venture.

"Honey, only rich women can afford to be shopkeepers, because most retail stores make no profit. So, I'm not sure what you're up to. It could end up costing you money you don't really have."

"Thanks Dad," I say. "Bye, see you soon."

Along with the thread and buttons comes a small kernel that will bloom into yet another daughter. I'm pregnant. The first people to know, besides the doctor, are the librarians and Susie. I wait a while to tell Scott. This is a surprise to me too, but I'm leery of his reaction to another child.

My two daughters, now 13 and 8, walk to the shop after school. Susie's kids too. And if we have a business meeting, we send them up to the Yellow Lizard for ice cream. People love the comfort and charm and beauty of the shop, a bit of a throwback to more innocent times. But sales are pretty slim. We break even the first year.

After Rowan is born at the local health clinic, I take a week off, and then bring her with me to the store. She's a pretty easy baby. Sometimes I tuck her baby bed in a shelf. Customers startle when they realize it's a live baby they see nestled amongst the fabric. And later, in nice weather, she shares a playpen outside with the son of the woman who owns the corner fish market. Small town safety net.

Since we're next to the library, if things get too boring during the business day, we go in there and peruse books or chat. And sometimes men amble by to say hello. I meet a man at Sewphie's who becomes very important in my life. My neighbor brings him in one day after they check out books from the library. He's charming and witty and has dimples and there's an instant flash—-I see it so clearly in my mind. Someday this man will be my lover. The blessings and curses of coming from an intuitive family!

The end of the second year we move to a bigger location across the street in an old white Victorian two-story house. The upstairs hosts my friend Joe's insurance business, and the side area we rent to a seamstress whose main customers are bachelors needing clothing repairs or rock musicians who want wild outfits made. She does pretty well, and her rent helps us. That year we order and re-order thread snippers. Unbeknownst to us they make perfect pot trimmers, and it's marijuana harvest time at the West Pole. We reap some of the harvest's benefits.

Susie is handling the books. I put together artful ads to run in the local papers, drawing liberally on old Dover arts and crafts books. We have wild text to appeal to our slightly wild customer base. We leave each other notes in our version of email in the early 1980's—a spiral bound notebook.

We put on a fashion show at Susie's with our customers as the models wearing the clothes they've made for themselves or their families from our fabric and patterns. It's a hit, but we run out of space for chairs. The second year we're more ambitious and ask Folkwear to help us put on a clothes show featuring their patterns. They are enthused and not only loan us their sample garments, but help to narrate the show. I write a fanciful and slightly goofy script tying the bold and broad ethnicity and styles of Folkwear together with a narrative thread. Once again, friends and customers model the garments. This time it's at Scott's and my house in the woods and we use the old deck that had been attached to Hi Ho Silver, our old trailer, as the stage. Over the stage Susie's husband rigs up a frame to hang a shade, a dramatic piece of the Christo fence, beautiful white nylon, floating softly on the afternoon breezes.

It reminds me of how surprised Scott, the girls and I were at that first view of the Christo Running Fence a few years before. Rounding a corner on Bodega Highway we nearly collided with the art fence that climbed up and down the hills of Marin and Sonoma Counties for two historic, artful weeks not far from where the fashion show takes place.

Somehow we get the local public TV channel interested and they produce a show two days in a row about the event with Susie and I and a representative from Folkwear. I have Rowan and her sisters dressed in Folkwear fashions, but Rowan, not quite one year old, wails up a storm. Scott has to take her out in the hall and comfort her, while Susie and I are interviewed. Countrified friends and neighbors have their 15 minutes of TV fame modeling the clothes. After we finish the show, they tell us to expect 400 people to come to our event, and we are shocked when they turn out to be right. Almost 400 people must be transported up the hill from Occidental via two vans. People, mainly women of all ages, but men as well, stand in the clearing in the redwoods on our land. Fortunately the weather is perfect and it's a party atmosphere.

"Who are those sophisticated people who just came in your front door?" a model asks me.

I look over to see my mom dressed in her finery, including high heels, an elegant hat, and a floaty dress that I'm sure she has made. Dad is wearing white, and an uncustomary Panama hat. Oh my.

"Those are my parents," I explain, somewhat surprised they haven't called to say they're coming. I show Dad where he can get a couple of folding chairs and they go outside to watch.

Another grandfather, Dennis Day from the Jack Benny show has come to see his young granddaughter in the show. He is visiting his son, who's our friend. It's all a little more than I expect, and for a minute I feel totally overwhelmed.

We sell food and patterns and provide a wine tasting. We get a name for ourselves when Gaye Le Baron, a local columnist, features the fashion show in the *Press Democrat*.

With a tone of disbelief (as in *it's so West County*) she describes the colorful day something like this: A model astride a horse rode in. Then a beautiful blond bride in a flowing gown walked in barefoot. Then a dark haired milkmaid, also bare foot, with milk pails slung over the pole from her shoulders, strolled onto the stage. Two robbers dressed in cowboy shirts held up another guy dressed in a Renaissance shirt. The strong box holds yet another Folkwear shirt and a cowboy strips off his own to put it on. And so on.

I guess if I were in the audience I would have gotten a kick out of it, too. But I am in the bedroom helping the models get dressed and out on the stage at the right time. It's hectic, but the guests love it and we've made our name synonymous with imagination, humor and beauty. Scott snaps pictures of the models, concentrating on the ones in the Victorian underwear. Later, when we look at the slides, that raven-haired milkmaid shows up in many of them.

We take in a new partner, Lynn, who brings in her husband's friend as a silent partner. Susie and I look forward to this infusion of money. I think that Susie is planning to leave the business, and this will make it easier for her.

Lynn shows up at the bank with a paper sack full of money that smells strongly of earth. It's from the silent partner.

"Wow, I hope nobody comes in to rob us right now," says the teller as she counts out $15,000 in hundred dollar bills. "Smells like this has been buried," she says, as she sniffs a thin bill and holds it up to the light. I'm holding my breath and wondering what the heck I've gotten myself into.

The third year we move the event to the Russian River

Vineyards in Forestville. The Vineyards has a large brick patio with a fountain, and in another building a tall replica of an old hop kiln, from the days when hops were grown here and harvested for beer. Susie, in old fashioned Folkwear undergarments, calls for help from a small window at the top of the hop kiln tower, and Joe, dressed in a red fireman's shirt and hat, runs to  her with a very tall ladder. He climbs up to the window of the hop kiln and throws Susie over his shoulder. Man to the rescue in red Folkwear Fireman's shirt.

There's flute and guitar music and a few booths with artisans offering crafted jewelry and carved and stitched leather pouches. They've paid us a small rental fee which we do not tell the Vineyards about. The chef offers ethnic finger foods for sale. It's sort of a mini-Renaissance Faire and it's a sell out.

We have so many reservations we have to schedule two shows for the day. We create a real buzz, but unfortunately fewer and fewer people sew, and we struggle to make our rent and pay for our merchandise. Susie is tired of it all and wants to move on to teach yoga and go back to school at Sonoma State.

The not-so-silent partner, who comes by every so often to say odd things, like: "I could buy three women just like you in Thailand."

"Oh," I respond.

I'm never sure what he means. Does this mean he likes me, or I'm a cheap floozy, or what?

I feel kind of like how I felt in the sixth grade. I'm mystified, clueless. Sometimes he backs me up against a wall and tells me he's carrying a hundred thousand dollars in the gem bag he has in his hand. I just smile and push him away.

"Oh, that's impressive. Be careful!"

"Don't worry," he says, "I've got plenty of big guys watching my back. Bodyguards. They're out there right now." He winks and gives me a clutching hug before he leaves.

At the rehearsal for the hop kiln show, he buys magnums of champagne for the models. And everyone drinks. He also offers some white powder, but all decline. It's a 1980s high time with the not-so-silent partner.

Lynn is a quilter and insists that quilting is becoming a big fad again, and we will make a fortune by moving the store to a bigger Santa Rosa location in historic Railroad Square. Susie gets the drift that this new partner will now be in control and quits. She has plans to get an advanced degree that will allow her to be a personal trainer.

Lynn and I rent a spot and start promoting. There will be a huge quilt show in Santa Rosa, and we want to be ready for it.

We put out a newsletter offering classes in quilting, in esoteric embroidery techniques, and crafty projects like making grapevine wreaths. We make friends with the new community of Hmong tribal refugees from Laos who bring in intricate and colorful needlework for us to sell.

A whole pile of their work is stolen, and I have to tell the men so they can tell their wives. We pay them for the stolen pieces. The women, influenced by quilting, start to include iconic symbols in their work, hearts and diamonds and more birds. The merging of two communities of creative women is exciting to watch.

Still, no matter how hard we try, we can't stave off the wolf at the door. A big competitor moves into town, a huge fabric shop from New York. We groan when we see their ad in the paper. My new partner Lynn is having even more serious marital difficulties than I am, and she's thinking of bailing and moving to Southern California. I'll be left holding the bag of dry goods and dealing with the not-so-silent partner.

Soon I'm in the same state as Lynn, leaving a marriage. I've got to find a job that pays me real money, not just in fabric for clothes. I've been making school clothes, prom and graduation dresses and shirts and ties, and my own pants and tops from the fabric, but fabric and thread won't pay for a place to live for the girls and myself. Scott has said many times, that if we ever split up, he will not be the one to move out.

I call my not-so-silent business partner and tell him to contact his lawyer and review his legal contract, and I ask him if he would like to take over the store. "Maybe I will do that, I think I know some girls who might like to run a store."

He sends in a beautiful woman, sensual, earthy and voluptuous, and completely stoned out of her mind. She sits with me and tries to take in all that is involved in running the business. Finally, she says, "It's way more than I thought. I just want to buy and sell stuff. And maybe sew some stuff."

That plan doesn't work out, so now I have the not-so-silent partner saying things over the phone like, "Don't ever walk in Santa Rosa without feeling afraid. I have someone who will rearrange that pretty little face of yours."

He leaves messages like these on my machine to what I thought was an unlisted number I have at the wine barrel house

I'm renting.

I call back, "I can't believe you said those things to me. We've been friends. What in hell is wrong with you!"

"I just want my money back. Maybe you can give me that diamond wedding ring of yours."

"Check your contract, contact your lawyer. I don't owe you a thing. Anyway, I think we may have laundered some dirty money!" I slam down the phone. Then I shake with a mixture of rage and fear, two emotions so closely and so often tied together in my life.

I hire a friend as my lawyer. The same man whose chickens I've run over with Sleeping Beauty. I tell him that if I suddenly disappear to suspect the not-so-silent partner who has threatened my life.

"Do you want to report him to the police?" my attorney asks.

"Hell no," I say,"But maybe get a restraining order?"

My new home is a rustic cabin with a large wine barrel attached as part of the house. It's all I can afford right now. On a vineyard, the property also has a bucolic acre devoted to vegetable gardens. I'm dating that man with the dimples. He tells me how to handle the not-so-silent partner, "Just say your boyfriend's a big burly biker with leather pants and a bad-ass temper." Man talk.

The so-called silent partner never makes good on his threats, even though every once in a while at the cabin I still come home to a message from him, and for years after, I keep running into him at music concerts and in cafes where he is super polite to me. Maybe when he looks at stocky Forrest, he thinks he might be a biker. Eventually the not-so-silent partner gets throat cancer and I feel bad because for a while I wished him dead. Next time I see him he speaks in a whisper. Not silent, but nearly.

Another woman and I take Sewphie's on the road to fabric shows. We sell patterns, one-of-a-kind buttons, embroidered hankies to fit into the artful child's dress pattern she has created and, which was featured in a prominent California magazine. We also sell whats left of bolts of material. We make and sell pieced clothing including shirts, dresses, and aprons for woman and children. But we tire of the schlepping, driving all over Northern California, and call it quits. Sewphie's has come to the end of the road. The chicken does not even want to cross over to the other side to see what's there.

The chicken sign is permanently retired. Years later I see it for sale in an antique shop.

Wine Barrel House

In that dreary wet winter of 1985, Scott and I take turns going to the Union Hotel bar. A couple of times a week, one of us stays home and helps the girls with their homework, and the other drives through the dark redwoods downhill into Occidental. As I drive, I'm careful to watch for animals crossing the road: deer, raccoons, foxes and so many rat-like, impossibly slow-moving possums. This year the roads are littered with dead possums, and local papers print recipes for things like "Road Kill Possum Stew." But I don't ever want to hit a possum. Or any animal.

Our destination downtown is the Union Hotel with its dark old-fashioned wood paneled bar, bottles stacked neatly on shelves like in a pub. It smells of stale beer, cigarettes and greasy raviolis, but the atmosphere offers hazy comfort, with a slight hint of danger.

The bartenders are amusing and upbeat. Several of them are friends. Our kids attend school together, we go to the same music events, share cookies and Christmas carols at the Union Hotel. Some have advanced degrees in psychology, Ph.Ds in communication. They're good at their jobs. The patrons are mostly male, but always a few women like me, eager for company and a break from home, willing to turn the *off* switch to *on*, the *on* switch to *off*. A change of scenery, a diversion, and sometimes, like at a dentist's office, the pain is numbed.

I never considered myself a barfly, even though it might seem like I was one in those days. But in the West County culture, the Union Hotel Bar and even Negri's across the street, are the closest we come to social halls. Everyone's a known factor, and often when a storm has brought down the power, it's warm and cozy. A generator thrums in the background. It's like other bars, with the posturing, the jukebox blaring. As a drinker, I'm a lightweight. Maybe a cheap date too. But I'm not looking for a date. In fact, I'm not looking at all. I'm shutting my eyes to all my problems here at the bar.

Sometimes he's growing a beard, and sometimes he's clean-shaven with dimples showing, but often this guy, Forrest, is also at the bar. He's the one I met early on at Sewphie's, when my little fabric shop was next to the library, before we grew bigger and moved across the street.

He did Rowan's astrological chart right after she was born and I've known him for five or six years now. I think he might like me. He's got an infectious laugh, and can always be counted on for an intelligent conversation. He's an avid reader, and I always learn something new from him, usually something scientific. For instance, he suggests I might like to read: *Gödel, Escher, Bach: An Eternal Golden Braid*. I try, and some of it interests me and some is too dense, or maybe I am.

But after a few drinks he's a man on a mission, and is just another bachelor, lonely and looking for a little company.

"I'm hungry for a Rocco burger in Freestone, want to join me?" he asks.

I think of the burgers, big, juicy, and greasy in a good way. Rocco's wife Maria bending over the counter, her big breasts practically bursting out into your face as she pours out the homemade Green Death hot sauce.

"No way," I say.

"I'm leaving for the Caribbean tomorrow, want to come along?"

I imagine tropical paradise, warm waters, no worries, Forrest's warm body next to mine. I think "yes," but say, "No thanks!"

"I'm going with friends to Petaluma to watch *Black Orpheus*, want to come?"

I can hear the samba beat, sense the magic of the movie set in Brazil. "No, are you kidding!"

I take it as kind of a running joke. Forrest knows I'm married, has bought insurance from Scott. They are the same age, both wear glasses, both totally nearsighted former athletes.

On my way back home from the bar I imagine how life might be with Forrest. He loves his work as a computer geek, he travels, he loves to read. He runs whitewater rivers in rubberrafts. He's been married a couple of times, like me, and he's charming. I'm a sucker for charm, but know from experience, it doesn't count for much in the big picture. Still, he seems caring and fun loving and there is a visceral attraction for me. It's that "chemistry" thing. Anyway, I have strong intuition, and I see it clearly even if he doesn't. I'm sure we will be a couple.

Everything changes the night that he invites me to go out to his car to listen to Brazilian music, I pause because I know deep

down that if I say yes, my life will never be the same.

I look him over, check out his hazel eyes, his stocky build, probably about six feet tall. He's wearing what must be his favorite outfit for the Union Hotel Bar, a blue tee shirt that says "Velikovsky's Right" in red on the front with a comet streaking across his broad chest. Over it he wears a plaid long sleeved wool shirt unbuttoned. It's patched at the elbows. A kind of nerdy woodsy look— somewhere between a professor and a lumberjack. He's eager, he's lonely. I'm the lucky recipient for this evening, but that doesn't really bother me because I'm eager, too, and I'm lonely, even if I am married. For once, I'm willing.

I close my eyes, like it's almost too much to look at him while I say, "Yes." All hell breaks loose from that night onward.

Scott becomes more and more difficult and demanding and probably senses something has shifted. Finally we have it out.

He's been on my case all night and in the morning when he gets up he says, "If you're not happy with me, just leave!"

"Okay then, I will!" I hear myself say this, but the words are not really connecting inside my brain yet. We slam doors and I pack a suitcase and tell the girls I will be gone for a few days. I'm not even sure where I'll go, but just know that I must go.

He lives up to his word, that if we ever separated, I would be the one to go, and the kids would stay with him. I leave behind all my dreams for a new start, a country home, built largely by my own hands, and a fertile garden. Most difficult, I have to leave my three girls for awhile.

Bitterness and accusations, betrayals, lawyers and bad letters written in despair follow, with unhappy kids and an unhappy spouse. Scott and I are separated, and it feels like slow death by drowning. We've been together 14 years. I'm leaving the known for the uncertain. Scott probably knows he deserves as much, but can't fathom that I'm really leaving him.

New love has its excitements, but pitfalls and surprises too. I'm having trouble putting the comfort of the familiar behind me in order to move on and Forrest and I are not exactly a solid couple, not yet, at least. He's shocked to hear that I have left Scott. I'm no longer the safe, flirty married friend. I think he's scared and so am I.

"Those women meant nothing to me," Scott screams into the phone. I'm staying at friends' houses where I sleep on the couch, or if I'm lucky, in a guest bed. My friend, Terry, pulls back the covers and leaves me a chocolate mint on the lace-edged pillow. Her tender care, and non-judgment are enough to dissolve me into tears. I'm suffering from lack of money and I really miss the girls and I'm a bit lost all the way around.

Scott cuts me off from our joint accounts and credit cards right away. I worry about the safety and health of the girls and am thankful the older two are 19 and 14, old enough to help out with five-year-old Rowan, but I know they all still need me.

I need money so badly I agree to work for Scott cleaning our own house. It's my chance to make sure the kids have clean rooms and clean clothes. And I can see them. As it is, he won't let them spend time with me and I have nowhere to take them except to friends' houses. I can't take them to Forrest's; I know how child custody battles begin. I miss my girls most at the beginning and the end of the day. It's so quiet without the morning noises with music playing on their radios, or sometimes Mary Lea practicing on the piano and singing, the coffee brewing, everyone running around getting ready for school. I miss hearing them talk on the phone to friends and miss snuggling with them in bed at night. They have been my main focus in life for years. When I go over to Forrest's, it's lonely and I'm sad but determined to change my life.

Scott is spiteful and drinking a lot. The girls report that he cries and plays certain music over and over, sometimes Elton John, or sometimes Stevie Nicks. And I hate to admit it, but I can't help worrying about Scott, too. I don't like being the source of pain. It feels very uncomfortable and not like I'd imagined revenge might feel. The water is about to cover my head. I'm about to sink.

I tell the girls, "This is the hard time. Everything will all work out soon, you'll see. Just be prepared. We live in a small town where people talk. They will ask a lot of questions which you don't have to answer! Just remember I really love you."

I trust my girls; I know my daughters to be strong, but no kid likes to be in this position. And neither do the parents. Here at the West Pole the gossip mill grinds, but on the other hand, there is support, and the unquestioned loyalty of friends.

My mother tells me that Scott has had his chance for heroism, but now that time is gone. "Move on," she whispers into the phone. She is not doing well right now, a recurrence of cancer.

I sell my diamond wedding ring to my brother and sister-in-law, so I have a little money to rent a cabin attached to a large wine barrel. The two buildings, a wine cask and a hand-built cabin, are hooked together by a roof, and when I look up, I see a little sunlight through a crack between the two. I know that when it rains, there will be a big leak. It's an odd and quirky arrangement that seems to suit me right now, and it's about the only place I can afford that is also on some property with some privacy. The new place is on a vineyard with several other rentals, a communal hot tub, a chicken coop full of hens laying eggs, and a lush vegetable garden that I work in and take food from. The landlady's freezer is stocked with homemade pesto, and that spring I live on a pasta diet.

The guy who's lived in the wine barrel house before me has left all of his junk behind. I discard syringes and plastic tubing, pack up photo albums of his wife giving birth—very personal stuff. I finish boxing up his belongings, and I spend a week cleaning, before the girls can come to stay.

I call him on the phone to say he can come pick up his stuff and he drives over about an hour later.

He removes the crystal door knob off the front door.

"This is mine," he shouts, "but I'm not taking anything else. I'll come by for these boxes later and just use my old furniture, I don't give a damn about it. I didn't want to leave here, and I hope the place burns to the ground!"

His Jeep spits out gravel from the driveway as he speeds off. His anger trails behind, tainting the place. The front door flops open in the wind until the landlady has it fixed. A new version of the crystal door knob, purple from sun, finally shines on the front door.

I call Mom and tell her, "It's pretty, and it's tiny, and it's not yet home, but it's mine for now." She's just happy to know that I have a roost, and a phone number and a spot for the girls, even if they have to sleep in an old wine barrel in a loft that smells like the barrels and vats I used to walk by to to get up to the wine tasting room where I worked for awhile. The loft smells like fermenting grapes when the girls lay down at night in their sleeping bags. Their clothes are rolled up and stored in large baskets on the floor. Almost all my furniture is still at the dream house.

Except for 19-year-old Grace, who's had a fight with Scott, the girls switch back and forth between my place and their dad's. Some evenings Grace stays with her boyfriend. It all seems clunky and hard to get used to. I'm at a low ebb in my determination to get a divorce. Not quite like "chewing on razor blades," as our mediator has described it, still the process is painful, just like the marriage counseling had been. And legally, it's painfully slow. Scott hasn't yet put the house on the market, and he hasn't even gotten the appraisals so I'll know what my share will be. I'm getting threatening calls from my ex silent business partner, and in general, the relationship with Forrest remains wobbly. I have a new friend, and sometimes we go dancing or he invites me for dinner and sends me home with his homemade chocolate chip cookies. But mostly I can't stop thinking about Forrest. He's captured me like a fish in a net.

The wood stove is constantly smoking, and on cloudy days the solar heat doesn't work, so there's no hot water. The girls and I often have to use an outdoor shower—not very private.

I've caught a neighbor peering in the window at Grace as she does ballet practice in the wine barrel room. I yell at him to stay away. I don't really feel safe here at all. Yet, the landlady brings over tomatoes still warm from the afternoon sun, flowers from the garden, and speckled green, copper and white eggs from a hen's nest in the coop. She says I should help myself to as much from the garden and the chickens as I need. She knows I'm on a budget. Her son is a toddler, and often pees on the chickens, until the rooster gets him right where it hurts, and he runs howling home.

Forrest decides to look for work in Brazil. He's still in love with the place. He applies for his work permits through a company interested in having him. We're a couple, but not much of one yet. This loose commitment we have bothers me and I tell Forrest that I'm not happy with the arrangement. Deep down, though, I still sense that we will be together for a long time. It's just in the cards, as my intuitive family would say.

I live for six months in the wine barrel house. I close *Sewphie's,* the fabric shop, and work a part-time job at the local community college. The work doesn't pay enough. I also teach textile arts and business skills at a vocational college. Finally, I get more regular work writing newsletters and planning events for several non-profit agencies, mostly in Santa Rosa. I commute in my truly funky green Toyota station wagon. I don't yet have a computer or even know how to use one, so everything is typed on an electronic typewriter in the wine barrel room. I also do a lot of odd jobs, including painting the exterior of houses on tall and rickety scaffolding. I get a job coordinating a big quilt and fiber arts show at the Marin County Fairgrounds and my boss is an impossible snob of a woman who sabotages my every effort. She also makes it clear that she pays her cleaning woman more than she's paying me. But I need the money. When I talk with Mom on the phone she says that this job is good for me, and it will bring other opportunities. I can tell from her shaky, hoarse voice that she's having a bad cancer spell. How I'd like to see her, but I can't afford the gas to drive down to Salinas. I still haven't settled my property with Scott. He has it all.

I just try to shut off feelings as much as possible, even with Forrest. I tread lightly. When I see a spider on the front ceiling lightly dangling, slowly letting itself down to the floor of the wine barrel house, I identify with it. Like the spider, I hang by a thread, cling to thin sticky filament.

Mom's cancer treatments are no longer working. My brother calls to say that she's losing weight and spends weeks at a time at the hospital sleeping. Forrest has planned a river rafting trip for his sons and me in Idaho and we're all at his Bodega Highway house ready to go. Bags and equipment are ready to load into his car in the morning. It will be a fun break from all this intensity, but since Mom is not doing well, the night before we're to take off, I call Dad.

"I think you'd better come down here," he says, "Mom might not last much longer."

"Wow, why didn't you let me know sooner? Should I come right away, or do you think a week will matter?" I ask.

"It might matter, I think you'd better drive down now," he says, hanging up.

I can't go on the rafting trip. I tell Forrest. He's mad and I'm upset too. By now I understand how much he hates a change in plans, and I've been looking forward to learning how to raft, and to leaving everything behind for wild waters. It's a disappointment to both of us and I don't like it that he's not very sympathetic to me and my sick mom. I wonder what this means for our relationship. I cry as quietly as I can. I don't want to disturb the boys, or make them wonder what is wrong. All they know so far is that I'm unable to go on the trip. All this is going on upstairs while downstairs in his office, Forrest's ex-wife and two of her children from a new marriage are spending the night. She will watch the place when Forrest goes.

I stay the night even though I'm not going rafting. Mainly,

I just don't want to be alone in the drafty wine barrel house, and I'm very upset about Mom. As I close my eyes, though, I have the most beautiful image of my mother, in one of her flowered hats, radiant smile. I can hear her hum, as she always hummed around the house as she worked. It soothes me into sleep.

After Forrest and the boys leave, I go back and rearrange my suitcase for the cooler weather of the Salinas Valley. I drive 101 for three hours to get to Mom and talk to myself out loud in the car, "I'm going to get real love this time, and settle for nothing less!" It's summer and hot. I roll the windows down and let my hair tangle into a knotted mess. I ponder what I need and want from a man this time. I become resolute. Forrest will have to come up to the mark.

I spend a week taking care of Mom, moving her out of the hospital, putting her on hospice and helping my dad sort through the logistics of dying so he can take care of her with the help of a very sweet and very pregnant hospice nurse. Mom moans or winces with pain every time Dad or I have to move her. She is skin and bones, less than 80 pounds. I sleep in bed with Mom and then take long walks so I can let the waves of emotion that have practically swallowed me, roll away into the pleasant golden vistas of the valley. Nature, always my solace. I sew head scarves to cover Mom's bald head, and make curtains to put around her bed for privacy. She and Dad are remodeling a small home and she sleeps in the living room, the bedroom not yet built. Her life with a builder will end as it began, with the sound of hammering and things just not as they should be.

"I'll think about you everyday, Mom," I say to her as I leave. "I mean every day of my life," I say kissing her. This, we both know, is our goodbye. She can barely talk, but opens her eyes and lifts her hand to hold mine. Life seems hard right now, very very hard. I drive the three hours home through heavy San Francisco traffic, and by the time I reach the vineyard, it's dark. With no streetlights to compete, the stars shine clearly,

Jupiter bright in the sky. I step from the car and inhale the familiar country fragrance.

I open the door to the wine barrel house and find my clothes, books and everything strewn all over the place. My landlord comes over. He explains that the previous tenant has taken all his furniture. I sit down on the floor to think. I call Scott. I practically scream orders to him over the phone.

"Get over here right now with my bed and that dresser that I've had since I was 16."

"Okay, okay, calm down, I'll be right over. Was your trip okay."

"No," I say, "and I can't talk about it right now."

I sit cross-legged, fold clothes and put them in piles. Then I go to the kitchen to pick up spices and dish towels and dishes, some broken. I await my bed, my dresser, my soon to be ex-husband. Sooner than I expect, I hear his truck on the gravel driveway. For once he does not disappoint.

Forrest has left a message on the machine to call him. "We're home, sunburned and happy, but I miss you. Call me as soon as you get this."

"Hi," I say, "it's me."

"Hi, love. How is everything?" He doesn't even wait for me to reply but says, "I'd love to see you, can you come over, or I can come there?"

"I'd like to see you too, but just not right now. Tonight I need to be by myself"

"You don't sound so good, are you sure you don't want to come over?"

"I'm sure," I say, not even wanting to say how I still have to set up my bed, put all the clothes into my dresser, clean up all the messes made in the kitchen, and bawl my eyes out. Something best done alone.

Into the Vale

Go down into the vale
into the blue-purple thistles.

Watch for thorns
catching your dress

Pulling you down
into the stickers, nettles.

Find the place deep in rosebuds
where three corners meet

And tumble into
the center of love.

Hanky Panky on Bodega Highway

Although it's less than 10 miles long, Bodega Highway looms large in my personal history. It's the road that connects the dots in my life at the West Pole with Forrest.

Forrest lived on Bodega Highway when I moved in with him. I was still married to Scott and life was messy. Out in front of the house hung a carved wooden sign: "Forrest and Sons." Forrest was a dad of two young boys, who were now in another state with their mom and step-dad. I found the sign endearing, it seemed that he was a family man who was not afraid to claim his fatherhood.

He rented out his garage as an auto repair shop, and in the past I'd brought old clunkers there to be fixed. Sometimes I wondered whether the VW camper would make it up the steep grade of O'Farrell Hill and into the garage driveway near the top. I never imagined that one day I would live here on Bodega Highway.

Forrest was still planning on moving to Brazil, but suggested that I move in with him.

"That wine barrel house is no place for you and the girls in winter," he said. "And even when I go to Brazil, you can stay. We'll work something out."

"Okay, I'll do it, but only if you're really sure, because I can't put my girls through any more changes, including their address," I answered

"I think the guest room would work for Mary Lea, and Rowan can have my boys' old room with the bunk beds. You and I will share a room of course!"

"Well, why not!" I said. By now we were full-on lovers. We were like rabbits, rutting goats, making love whenever and wherever the urge struck us. New love in its sensual glory.

We'd agreed on a time and date for me to move in. I boxed up belongings and stacked furniture in the station wagon to take over to Forrest's like we'd planned, before dinner time. I kept calling, and calling but he wasn't home. Finally, feeling mad, disappointed and abandoned, I decided to blow it off and go to a Labor Day party at good friends. I got home very late, 3 am, but there were messages on the answering machine:

The first one was short: "Hi, It's me, Forrest. I've cleared out half the dresser for you, and put fresh sheets on all the beds. I hope I'll see you here tonight." The second one just asked, "Where are you?" and the third one finally said the good stuff: "I love you, and I'm glad you're moving in with me. I think you and the girls will like it here." No mention of where he'd been or why he didn't call earlier. I went to bed feeling torn. I hoped I wasn't making another mistake. The next day I drove over with all my stuff. There was a note pinned to the door, *Come on in and get comfortable. I'll see you soon, Forrest.* I had to lug my clothes and some of my furnishings down to the front porch. Get out the key from its hiding place and go in. I looked the place over with a more critical eye. He had cleared out the dresser, like he said and I put my purse and some of my clothes in what had been his bedroom, but at least for now, would be ours. I was happy that the girls liked Forrest now and they were eager to have bedrooms that were more like what they were used to and not the crazy loft of the Wine Barrel House.

The bathroom was tiny and only had a bathtub with no shower. There was a small living room and kitchen, all the walls covered in knotty pine. Forrest had oak antiques in the rooms and quilts from his grandmother and mother on the beds. It was a cozy place at the edge of a forested property with a year-round spring that provided water. He had a downstairs office in the basement.

"If the boys want to come live with us, we could turn the office into a bedroom for them," he suggested casually. Oh my, I hadn't even considered that possibility. Five kids with two adults in a new relationship? Doubt nagged at me, but I'd chosen my path and an explorer rarely turns back.

"Make it your own," Forrest told me, "feel free to put some of your things around. Really, I want you to." But I'd observed this man, and merely hung up one ruffled fabric-covered swag light, cleaned piles of computer magazines from the floor and off the couch, and added a rocking chair. The rocking chair I had used when the girls were little and I read books to them, or rocked them through a hard night.

When he came home from work Forrest said, "I've been attacked by the *Ladies Home Journal!*"

I laughed, but knew I'd been right to go slow.

He was a guy who liked to be in charge. I moved in with a lion, a rather fussy lion, and stepped with caution. He showed me how he liked the toilet paper so that it rolled toward the outside, and he said that I should just let his housekeeper wash the girls and my things. Twice in the heat of summer-time I made popcorn and burned the pan. The housekeeper left Forrest a note. She quit. Her life had been easier without us and our messes.

At this beginning of our relationship, we often drove the highway into the little town of Bodega to eat at the Bodega Schoolhouse, which was an important setting for Hitchcock's film, *The Birds*.

In those olden days, the Schoolhouse was the best and the first of the California cuisine gourmet restaurants in West County. A delicious meal always awaited just a 10-minute cruise down Bodega Highway. We would smooch and cuddle as we sat side by side, wallowing in our newly-announced love. We were horny forty-year-olds. There was Hanky Panky on the Bodega Highway.

To get to the Schoolhouse Restaurant, we always passed another school. Unused for years, the school was now a part of the regional park system. Watson School stood on the south side of the highway, just where the Christo Fence hiking trail begins.

What I remember now when I pass by the Watson school is the youngish couple who, on a naughty night, stopped and made love on one of the picnic tables after dark, in a light rain. They just couldn't wait for the 10-minutes to home. Shortly after, the park put up a fence, a gate, and a sign, "Watson School—Gate closes at sunset!"

Forrest and I talked it over and agreed that I would clean the place and Forrest would pay me and then I was to pay him a small amount for rent. It seemed straightforward enough, but I guess I'd expected something a little more gallant. Where was my prince? He also still defined his lifestyle by nightly visits to the Union Hotel bar to hang out with his cronies. Sometimes the girls and I would join him at the Hotel for a dinner of spaghetti

and meatballs, but still, I didn't feel right about how much time he spent there and how much beer he drank. I wondered, was this really love? But he was a good lover and made me feel desired and wildly satisfied.

When I first moved in, the refrigerator was filled with beer and mayonnaise. The pantry was sparse, only ketchup, paper towels and cans of tuna on the shelves, so Forrest and I drove Bodega Highway into town to shop for groceries. People stopped to talk to us. Most of them knew the story, but they were discreet and no one seemed to judge or snub us. We survived our first public appearance together. Next we attended a play at Rowan's school and sat in the audience holding hands. Our declared coupledom had begun for real.

The entryway to Forrest's home was a mess of cracked and missing tiles, and I started to repair it. I just couldn't help myself. It's in my DNA to want to get my hands on building supplies and to fix things up. This urge applies to men as well as houses. I've learned that tiling a floor is way easier than a man project.

While I worked in the hallway, I found a sign, "Nubian Stud Service, $15.00."

"What's the deal with this sign?" I asked

"Oh this place used to have goats," Forrest answered from the other room.

"Are you keeping this goat sign, or can I toss it?"

"Just scratch out 'Nubian' and change the '$15.00' to '$20.00' and hang it back outside the house," he said laughing.

I didn't laugh, even though I got the humor. Bachelor ways die hard. I tucked the sign up high on a dusty shelf in the downstairs basement outside his office door.

One day the soon to be ex, Scott, burst in the front door without even knocking.

"Show me your room," he insisted.

"No, you've got to leave!" I said.

My mind whirled back to a time when I'd had to call the cops on my first husband, soon after we separated.

"Aw, don't worry, I'm not going to hurt you, I just want to see where you are," Scott said, pushing me aside.

Finally after saying nothing more, he left. I was trembling and wondered why the men I've been with have had such a hard time letting go, when it seemed like they'd let go of me long before I left them.

A few months later, Scott called. "Your dad called to say that your mom died. He wants you to call him back." Then he hung up.

Dazed, I sat by the phone not knowing what to do. Sputtering and crying and wondering how I'd gotten here to Bodega Highway where no one was home to hug me or tell me that everything would be all right. Mom had always done that. And I was surprised at Scott's gruffness, I know he loved my mother too.

After 25 years of cancer and cancer treatments, and silent suffering, Mom was gone. Losing her struck me down into a deep grief.

When I called Dad back, he said he had lost my new phone number at Forrest's and had broken the news to Mary Lea and she passed on the news to the rest of the family at Scott's. Later in the day, Mary Lea called crying. She'd been asked to sing "Somewhere over the Rainbow," and she didn't know if she could do it.

"Your grandmother wanted that and she knew you would be able to do it." I assured her. But I wondered how we would all get through the memorial.

The next day, my wine barrel house landlady called.

"The wine barrel house is completely destroyed," she said, "burned down to the ground. A terrible fire. We think it was caused by the new wood-stove in the wine barrel, but it's all gone, every stick and stave. All just charcoal now." She let out a big sigh before she hung up.

So much bad news at once. I was relieved that the girls and I weren't in the wine barrel house when it caught fire, and I was relieved that finally Mom was out of pain.

Scott agreed to take the kids down to Carmel for her memorial service and I would meet them all there. I didn't feel I could comfort the kids, I wasn't settled enough myself for that.

Forrest, we decided, wouldn't come. "You don't have the emotional reserve for any more drama," he said. I realized he probably didn't either. I think this was way more than he expected when he first invited me to listen to Brazilian music in his car in front of the Union Hotel.

At the memorial I sat next to Dad, who shook the entire time. "Your mother told me not to shake or cry," he said. "She knew I would." The impossible demands of the dead, of couples, simply impossible expectations. Mary Lea and my nephew performed beautifully, but both of them choked up. My brother had to take his youngest son out of the church because he just wailed the whole time. Rowan who was the same age was more stoic, and Grace, delicately beautiful and looking more the young woman sat quietly a few rows behind all of us. Scott seemed sad too, Mom had a soft spot for Scott, even though she understood only too well the problems in our marriage. For once we were civil to one another. He gave me a big hug and said how sorry he was to lose "our Maga." Our relationship was finally turning a corner.

The following Thanksgiving, Forrest and I bravely and rather brazenly invited family—our kids, my brother and sister and their kids, and my father to celebrate. It was our first Thanksgiving together as a couple. For my family, it was a sad one—our first without Maga.

Close to twenty of us spilled out around the table laden with turkey and all the trimmings, including an Ozark Pudding made by Forrest from his family's recipe. His mom in Missouri had shared the recipe over the phone. Normally he didn't cook a thing, and I was touched that he'd pitched in on this special day. It showed me that he cared and he would help out.

Ozark Pudding is a simple apple cake with lots of brown sugar. The Ozarks, like here, has lots of apple trees. When the cake came out of the oven Forrest turned to Grace.

"I can't remember, is the toothpick supposed to come out clean or gooey when it's cooked?"

I heard Grace answer: "I have no idea. When Mom's cooking we usually just wait for the smoke detector alarm to go off."

The yin and yang of food in my kitchen, either blackened or not cooked enough. I cringed.

As it turned out, everyone was happily noisy and the food eagerly consumed, and we ended up, at Rowan's urging, playing Pictionary and laughing into the night.

I was still married and trying to work my way through an amicable divorce with both of us using the same mediator. It was a slow go and we weren't always polite. Heated words were exchanged and Scott recorded everything. He said it's because he has a bad memory, but I thought it was because he was trying to trick me somehow. Neither of us trusted the other, but at least we weren't shouting all the time, hurling accusations at each other. He told me he had started to date.

Grace had moved to Los Angeles with her boyfriend, who seemed nice enough, but didn't promise much of a future. I understood her reasoning though. Why stick around a chaotic mess with a community that watches to see what will happen next in the local soap opera?

My other two daughters divided their time between their Dad's house and Forrest's and my house. In first grade, Rowan was the butt of teasing. She was called, among other things, "noodle head" for her super curly hair. Sometimes when I picked her up at Harmony School for our days together, she looked unkempt. Her clothes were kind of dirty and ratty and her hair not brushed. Although I knew what a chore it was to brush through that golden curly hair, I blamed Scott for neglecting her. Maybe he was depressed but I felt that his self pity and his drinking habits were getting in the way of his parenting.

Finally, Scott arranged for a woman to live in her camper in the driveway of our dream home in exchange for taking care of the kids when it was his watch. She burned candles in all the windows and it scared the heck out of me. She made beaded jewelry to sell at Grateful Dead concerts. But the girls liked her, and that was most important to me. Whenever I left my old dream house for Forrest's I'd feel a deep sentimental sadness. I'd let go of my hopes, my dream house. My life had changed completely and sometimes at Forrest's when I looked in the mirror, I didn't even recognize myself.

Scott sold our house and gave me the small amount of money he said was my half. We were divorced. My second time, his first. I knew that now I was faced with taking a hard look at my part in the failure of this second marriage, as I hoped to not take the problems into my new relationship.

Forrest's two sons, 12 and 14, moved in, and my three daughters all wanted to live with us so we looked for a bigger house on an offshoot of Bodega Highway. We were not yet married and had no wedding plans, but we decided to pool our money and buy a house together. Even though Forrest put in three times as much money as I did for a down payment, he was fine with my being on the title.

Like a small dormitory, the new house had enough room for everyone and for years was a buzzing beehive. Five kids and multiple friends who spent the night, everyone with different tastes in music. Bob Marley, Elton John, and the heavy metal screeches of Black Sabbath wailed from the bedrooms. Mary Lea and Rowan had piano lessons while the boys played their guitars, Rick and Ron their respective teachers.

I took refuge in quiet, tree-lined places to walk, sometimes cutting through a wide organic farm with berries, including bright round red currants in fall, and plentiful leafy green produce, bordered with a wild array of sunflowers in summer. Everyone said it was okay to cut through, and the organic farmer's daughter was in the kids' school car pool. There was a lot to like about the new place, except where the driveway came out at the top on Occidental Road, right at Dead Man's Curve. We had three teenagers learning to drive. We nearly got clipped a few times and had to teach defensive driving skills, and how to floor it when needed. Fortunately, we all survived, with our sanity and our cars mostly intact.

Buying the house together represented a turning point, a big risk and commitment for the two of us. We had combined our kids for better or for worse. Now that I think back on it, it was a very brave, and mostly foolish, thing to do.

As it turns out, the kids liked each other, even though the boys found six-year-old Rowan annoying. She told on the older kids. "Mom, they're smoking out in back." she tattled. "Mom, Kevin got a real tattoo—as in r-e-a-l," she screeches down the hallway. "Mom, Lee just climbed out the window—he's sneaking off," she'd shout from the bottom of the stairs. "Mom, Mary Lea's boyfriend is in her bedroom."

Grace returned from Los Angeles. She'd broken up with her boyfriend, but she was hardly at home: she sold jewelry at a Santa Rosa department store and studied at the local community college. Soon she transfered to Cal Poly in San Luis Obispo and never lived in Sonoma County again. I missed her and we talked on the phone a lot. Forrest didn't understand why we needed to talk so much. "It's just what mothers and daughters do!" I tried to explain to him.

"But you know," he said, "our nest is far from empty."

Years later, when all five kids were gone, I walked around in a daze, trying to fathom life without all the demands and joys, the commotion and constant activity of full family life with kids at home. For years afterward I made too much food for dinner, and we'd dine on leftovers for days. The Mom thing goes down hard.

Magic for Paulo

Occidental is a magical place, but for a few years in a row our Brazilian friend, Paulo, always seemed to arrive just in time for something amazingly magical in our little town. Paulo was Forrest's boss for a while, a long virtual commute from Occidental to São Paulo, Brazil. Even though Paulo is no longer his boss, now he visits as a friend, spending a few days with us after completing business in San Francisco. He imports computer software and video games to Brazil. He uses his Occidental visit as a de-stresser before getting back onto a plane for the more than 14-hour trip home to São Paulo. I think too, he still hopes Forrest will change his mind and come back to work for him, this time in Brazil. "You can work in Rio, or anywhere you like it." Paulo always leaves with this same offer.

One year Paulo comes just before Thanksgiving, that holiday peculiar to the United States, featuring turkey, something Paulo's never eaten before. On this holiday we have only one of our five children spending the day with us, my youngest daughter Rowan. The other kids are with their other families. A friend, Cary, invites us for the Thanksgiving meal; it's to be a rather large gathering of friends in his backyard in Camp Meeker, the next town down Bohemian Highway.

Paulo can't believe the feast set before us. The turkeys, plump and brown— some cooked on barbecue, some hot out of the oven. Also tofu formed into a turkey shape ("tofur-key"), for vegetarians. Bowls of candied yams with marsh-mallows on top, mashed potatoes, gravy, green beans with onions, mushrooms, several versions of stuffing—rice with pine nuts, bread with onion and celery, even one of corn-meal. There are whole cranberries, and jellied cranberry from the can, pumpkin and mince pies, lemon meringue pies and chocolate and carrot cakes. Paulo has never eaten half these things before. It's all new.

"What is this?" he points at the pumpkin pie.

"Calabasa—squash pie," I answer. He frowns and laughs.

We start the feast with hands held round a very long set of coupled tables and individually say what we're thankful for. This takes a little time and patience because all the food smells so good—aromas of cinnamon and sage, butter and sugar and yeasty bread rolls. About 30 people are ready to chow down and Paulo is one of them.

At the conclusion of the meal, we sit around in the filtered sunlight under redwood trees drinking a little more wine and talking, and then the music begins, rock and roll. Some guests have brought guitars and drums. We get up and dance. We shake our tail feathers, expanding out into the late sunshine on the deck above Dutch Bill Creek. The slightly skunky smell of pot wafts through the air. A few dancers do interpretive twirls and leaps and kicks and dance like there's no stuffing in them. Rowan and all the other kids dance too. Paulo's eyes are round, his smile very big. "So this Thanksgiving?"

"Not really the usual for us," I start to explain.

"I like this Thanksgiving very much! I really like it. So special!" Paulo exclaims.

"And the squash pie sweet and good. You have nice friends. Occidental is special in all of California," Paulo says.

The next year Paulo has again come for a computer conference followed by a stay with us. At night, in our Bodega Highway house, before all our children moved in with us and we had to get a bigger house, I can see the glow of a computer screen under the door. He's working I think or maybe just jet lagged and unable to sleep. He's brought a lot of cash with him—over $10,000, he says, and he has it hidden somewhere in the room; we don't want to know where! I can't seem to sleep, either.

That night Forrest comes home from his work—his new job after quitting Paulo. "There's a rumor in town that two guys at the Union Hotel bar won a big lottery ticket, $10,000, and they don't want to claim it because they are in the underground economy and want no government connections," Forrest tells us.

"What this underground economy?" Paulo asks.

"Pot farmers—marijuana growers," Forrest adds when Paulo looks a little confused.

Paulo gets it and bursts out laughing. "So now what shall happen?"

"Well, supposedly Danny, the owner of the bar, bought the ticket at a discount and the guys want to buy the town a drink. There are all kinds of bets going on, and Danny bet that they would not be able to serve $1,000 worth of drinks in one hour. If they don't, the guys owe him the balance, but if they do, all drinks after that would be on the house!"

"Let's go," we all say in unison.

It's winter and dark out at 6 pm. Still we see a big line snaking out in front of the Union Hotel. We get in it and soon are in a row of people about six rows back from the bar, against a wall. There are probably over a hundred people in here, way over the limit, but in our town, the firefighters are volunteers, and they're here too! Even the fire chief wants to see this.

"So many people!" Paulo exclaims.

"Yeah, I'll try to make it up there. Let's decide what we want," Forrest says.

"It's cold, I'll have a hot brandy with a lemon twist and sugar," I say.

"Beer for me," Paulo says.

Former bartenders, are leaping over the bar to help make the drinks. They are just barely keeping up.

After about 30 minutes of this, Danny does not even ring up the drinks; he knows he's lost the bet. He'll be hosting the town to drinks, too.

There are lots of toasts. "To our hosts," one gent says. "To our hosts," We answer, not really wanting to give away their identity. I look over at Paulo, practically crushed into the wall, foam flying from his beer. He catches my eye. Paulo just laughs. "Occidental special place on the earth!" He says shaking his head.

Next time Paulo comes for a brief visit. In the morning he has to leave for the airport, we take him to breakfast at Howard's Station Cafe, named for the place the train used to stop in Occidental. In the midst of our meal, a guy in a black suit, with top hat, gets up.

"I have to perform a big magic show tonight and I need to practice my tricks. Would any of you mind watching? Any objections to a magic show?" he asks.

There are murmurs, but hey, it's Occidental. He's at the West Pole. People living on the shaky edge of the continent practically as a chorus say, "Yes, do it."

"Yes, I'd love it, love it," I say clapping maybe a little too enthusiastically. Mary Lea and Rowan give me the stink eyes, as in, MOM!

"OK," he says, taking off his hat as he starts in on a very quiet series of tricks. Flowers appear from his hat at the wave of his wand, even a rabbit appears. Coins on every finger and then *poof*—gone. And he pulls coins from our ears, our hair, from Paulo's sleeve cuff. Cards are cut in half and reassembled. Ropes grow up to the ceiling and fall back to the floor when he yells, "Down!" I've completely forgotten about my Belgian waffle. My tea is cold. I'm mesmerized and happy. Mary Lea loves it too and finally gives me a smile. Rowan is still trying to figure out the last trick. He doesn't explain or do much of what must be the verbal part of his act, just the plain old ordinary magic with a few commands. I am ecstatic.

"Paulo, I have a secret love for all magicians. For example, I'm in love with this guy right now. I'd follow him anywhere."

Forrest laughs. He knows about this special love. And I'm thinking the magician very handsome, tall, slim, with dark hair and eyes and a quick hand! My theory—magicians make excellent lovers!

"What Forrest says about this secret love?" Paulo asks in his lovely Brazilian Portuguese accent.

"He knows." I wink at Paulo.

"Occidental is very special place on all the planet, maybe universe," he says laughing. And today, as every day, I have to agree with him.

Play the Blues at Our Wedding

It was our wedding day and I was running around taking care of all the details, a bit frantic, and very nervous. The cool foggy morning with soft light filtering down through the tall trees calmed me, but I still had a lot to do. I'd hired Sharon, daughter Grace's multi-skilled friend, to help me with the table decorations, the flowers and food, and we were winding flowers through a rented arbor when Forrest and the boys stopped by. They had come to get started on setting up chairs, but right away Forrest felt a desire, a need to micromanage what I'm doing. "Don't you think you should wait to put out the greenery? Where is all the food going anyway? Where's the bar going to be?" Well, I thought, maybe he just wanted to be helpful and genuinely wanted to know about the food and the bar. But, his traffic director behavior meant he was just as nervous as I was. We were getting married after living together for five years.

After I asked him to marry me, and he'd said, "Yes!," we decided to do it as quickly as possible, before either of us had time to think about it too much. We'd each tried marriage twice before and it hadn't worked. But by now we'd combined our kids and bought a house together, and in most respects, were already operating as a family. We wanted to formalize things and we hoped neither of us would chicken out at the last minute.

After considering a lot of options, we found an outdoor place called Chenoweth Woods not far from where we were living. It was in a densely wooded area with a place to arrange chairs for a ceremony. There was a kitchen of sorts, and a cement dance floor. Much to my surprise it turned out that the Chenoweths were my distant relatives on my mother's side and they gave us a good cousin discount. I'd asked colleague Joyce Chong to pick an auspicious "Chinese Long Life Happiness" date for our wedding and it turned out to be Sunday, July 29th.

Barbara, a crystal dealer and former neighbor, offered to start off the wedding ringing Tibetan chimes, "to clear all harmful vibrations from the area." This was going to be a do-it-yourself West County wedding.

My 74-year-old dad would walk me, the non-virginal 49-year-old-bride, down the aisle. I had picked out an outfit with a Victorian flavor—a wide brimmed, veiled hat decorated by my former Wine Barrel House landlady. And a creamy white, lacy dress. Ironically the designer label read, Scott McClintock. The two older girls and I often ventured into San Francisco to his wife, Jessica McClintock's Gunne Sax outlet store looking for prom and other fancy high school dresses. Grace, Mary Lea and Rowan would wear variations on the theme of pinks, purples and peach. Mary Lea and Grace had chosen their own clothes, but I'd picked Rowan's and she didn't like it. I had to soak it in a bath of tea to tone down the stark white background. It didn't fit her quite right, but she was a sport and wore it and along with some white Mary Jane shoes she didn't care for, either. The boys and Forrest rented tuxedos, shirts and shoes. We had to get one pants leg split for Kevin to accommodate his cast. He had broken his leg a few days before at a party. "Wrestling," he explained.

Dad, looking very spiffy in a white jacket, slacks, long-sleeved dress shirt with tie, brought Veola with him. She was his girl-friend and once had been my mother's vivacious, attractive high school friend. Veola and Dad reconnected after finding out that they both had lost their spouses. When they were dressed, Veola in navy blue and white, they called the dormi-tory house and told us we could use their room at The Inn at

Occidental. We drove down and parked, went upstairs with our arms full. Ladies need make up, combs, fancy underwear, and to lay their outfits on a big bed.

When we went upstairs we were all excited and pleased to be dressing in swanky surroundings. The room was big and had a balcony. There was a king-size bed with carved headboard, and a long, antique oval mirror, in which we checked ourselves out, once we were ready. The older girls encouraged Rowan, told her she looked, "cute" and "nice." Forrest and the boys got dressed at home and planned to meet us at the wedding site. Old fashioned idea—the groom shouldn't see the bride in her finery before the wedding.

Outside the Inn, our friend Carl waited in his white jeep—carefully washed for the occasion—so he could drive us ladies to the woods for the wedding. I was so nervous the girls suggested I have a shot of whiskey or something. Grace called the front desk and they sent up a complimentary bottle of champagne. Woohoo, let the good times roll! Our friend Diana knocked at the door. She had made the wedding bouquets — mostly roses—and she handed a flower girl's basket of petals to Rowan.

When we arrived I looked at my three daughters. Grace at 24 was finishing up college, Mary Lea, 19, was working at a retail store that featured kits for making dolls, toys and clothes, and she was singing in a band. She had just moved back home with us. Rowan was 10, funny and serious at the same time with a gift for writing. She had recently won a Schwinn bike for an essay. The boys, still teenagers, and attending a local alternative high school looked handsome all cleaned up. Kevin was about to move in with his mom and her family. Lee was saving money to move out. His passion was mountain bike racing and he had a job building bikes. All of the kids had survived this transition into a new family.

Forrest and the boys, with help from some of the guests, had finished setting up chairs, and the guitarist had arrived and was practicing, music bouncing off the redwoods. In the audience sat my ex, Scott, with his new wife and baby, and nearby was Forrest's former wife with her new large family. Old friends from the beginnings of my life in Occidental were seated, along with my siblings and their families, a cousin and her husband, Forrest's young brother from Texas, colleagues from work, people from the Union Hotel, people who had started local communes, and so many teenagers and their parents. They were all there to witness our marriage. It was a splendid cross-section of our lives at the West Pole.

Our friend George Z, the guy Forrest called the Pope of Occidental, with his silver hair, tanned complexion, and booming voice, married us. George was once a San Francisco attorney and Forrest had invited him to add some words if he felt like it. For a minute during the ceremony, Forrest lost his voice. People laughed, but I tensed up. Was he scared to say the vows we wrote together so carefully, or was he filled with sentiment? Then as I started repeating my vows, I realized the Pope had changed them and had us repeating the old fashioned ones that included "in sickness and in health," and to "love and obey." That's what The Pope had decided to add. I turned red but proceeded to parrot back the Pope's vows, looking hard at Forrest, who was oblivious to any changes in words. Soon we were both focused on not running screaming back up the aisle saying, "No, I just can't do it again!"

Mary Lea sang one of my favorite songs, made famous by Bette Midler: "The Rose." The lyrics, touch on the dangers of love, but end with the hopeful image of love as a seed that will bring forth bloom in the springtime. It seemed to fit. Mary Lea's soulful rendition brought a few people, including me, to tears. She was accompanied on guitar by Doug, Director of the Occidental Community Choir. The wedding pictures showed an incredible ray of light shining down through the woods and right on Mary Lea as she sang the song. It was, I have to say, a magical wedding, even if the kids were all a bit sad, giving up any hope of their original families reuniting once again. They were troopers and stood up there for and with us in the sun-filled forest.

I'd arranged for a friend, Debbie, to take photos, and she was willing to trade a painted silk wearable art outfit for the shoot. Like my mom had done, Debbie was doing her best to survive recurring breast cancer. She'd made it for eight years so far. She was upbeat and had the chutzpah to direct us for the pictures. Scott's wife and another wedding guest also took pictures. We were soon tired of getting our pictures taken—we all wanted to start the party!

Remembering the way we had begun that fateful night at the Union Hotel bar, maybe we should have picked Brazilian music, sambas and bossa novas dance music, but we picked the blues. Nick Gravenites, renowned rock-blues player from the heyday of the Paul Butterfield Blues Band, Electric Flag, and Quicksilver Messenger Service. Nick and his wife Marcia were local friends. Blues music seemed to us the perfect accompaniment for our wedding celebration. We already knew that marriage was not always about hot sex, and slow romantic dancing cheek to cheek.

Forrest, not much of a dancer, did the obligatory first dance, and then I danced with my dad, and with my best friend through life, Bob. My sister Diane said, "Too bad about the music, it's not that good for dancing," but we loved it and later, after a few glasses of champagne, Diane was out there dancing too. Nick

generously let our son Kevin play a heavy metal riff and then my nephew Michael got up and used Nick's guitar to play and sing "Little Red Rooster." We couldn't have been happier as the day melted away. We barely had time to eat the delicious

food brought by our friends, by our community, including a full salmon caught and prepared by our friend Elmer and a cornucopia of fruit, artfully arranged by Patti, one of my first friends and neighbors. She had blueberries spilling out across the table. The cake was chocolate with raspberry filling, made by Joleen, whose brother was the Fire Chief of the volunteers from Occidental. When we cut the cake, Forrest and I were nice to each other. We were a mature couple who didn't try to smear cake onto each other's faces. We wanted to eat the cake, savor the chocolate.

We left the wedding at dusk in a shower of birdseed, more friendly to the local birds than rice, we were told. We knew that our friend Agnew, who didn't have much money but had a big truck, would make good on his wedding gift to haul all the garbage and recyclables to the dump. Another friend would get our family to fold up and stack all the chairs and rented equipment. We were duty free for the evening as the boys' uncle had volunteered to keep an eye on things at home. Of course he was the same one who hooked up with the woman bartender we'd hired, giving the teenagers full reign of the bar for the rest of the evening.

We had a very brief honeymoon which consisted of dinner at River's End in Jenner where the Russian River connects to the Pacific Ocean, followed by a night at the Inn at the Tides in Bodega Bay. When we left we saw that the room was filled with birdseed fallen from our wedding clothes The next day when we returned home we found evidence of continued partying, with a few patches of vomit outside and crushed empty beer cans carefully stacked next to the recycling can in the garage.

That night we snuggled together in our own bed and looked at each other. We'd made it this far, surely we could keep on. "Goodnight my sweet," Forrest said. "Good night husband." *Husband*—the word felt kind of good and not nearly as scary as I thought it might.

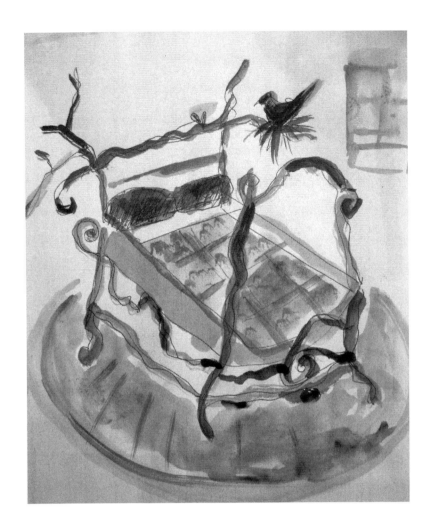

Ruby Slippers That Look Like Clogs

"I paint because I need to, and I paint whatever passes through my head without any other consideration." —Frida Kahlo

I'd been using my half of the garage to paint silk scarves and hang them to dry on lines crisscrossing below the sticky cobwebs of black widows. Next to me, stepsons Lee and Kevin and their guy friends played War Hammer, each describing how his character will kill the other kid's character and with what weapons. They'd transformed a former ping pong table into a set for the daily war they carefully orchestrated. As with all wars, it had rules to be followed.

Art has only a few rules, and you can break them as often as you like.

I'd washed each scarf in cold water and then ironed it dry in order to set the paints and dyes, then I carefully folded them, pinned on a small copper colored card with washing instructions and color-sorted them into silk piles. I finished my biggest order, 60 hand-painted scarves for two Nordstrom

department stores. I was burned out, but the ladies in Walnut Creek and Corte Madera would have a colorful array of silk scarves to pluck through and hopefully purchase.

Forrest's parents had driven from Kansas City to take their grandsons panning for gold, except that now Roger's mom was staying with us and sleeping in our bedroom. She wasn't feeling so well. Her blood pressure was high. We fixed our bed so the head was elevated.

In time for the grandparents visit, Kevin shaved off half his hair. The other half of his head was still covered with long golden curls. The grandparents had been warned, and when they arrived and first saw him, they didn't flinch; they said absolutely nothing about the hairstyle. Forrest's dad packed the boys into a station wagon and off they went in search of real gold.

Forrest's mom and I worked together in the garage making scarves. She seemed to enjoy herself, painting and stamping on scarves to take home as gifts to her sisters, Forrest's aunts. After the boys got home, we made a big family dinner and then the grandparents got into the station wagon and drove off, back to Kansas City, Missouri.

Shortly after the grandparents visit, Forrest caught me in the kitchen and turned me around to face him. "I just got a bonus check and I think we should use it to build a studio for you." I couldn't believe it. I hugged him tight, gave him a kiss and glowed with anticipation. A dream of years would come true!

The process of planning and building, two of my favorite pursuits, began again. Carpenters hammered and sawed, the noise reverberating into the redwoods, up the canyons. My eighty-year-old dad, who had moved to Sebastapol, came over to check it all out. He'd never gotten building out of his blood. "Inspector Clouseau is here," the carpenters liked to tease him. He took the teasing in stride—familiar building site humor. Mary Lea had surgery to remove polyps from her sinuses and sat outside watching the guys work, with a big bandage over her face. Watching the carpenters, some of them young men, was a diversion for her. We made cookies for them and happy carpenters whistled while they worked.

It was finally finished. Painted green, with a ramp railing made from redwood branches, and a skylight all the way down the center. The ramp was important, I was working with disabled students at a local community college and wanted art access for everyone.

I just couldn't believe it. As I walked the length of the new studio, I teared up. "You're not going to cry again!" Grace said. "Oh let her cry if she feels like it!" the more emotional Mary Lea chimed in. I've wanted a studio most of my life, and my life has stretched on for fifty years now to this day of the first real studio. I felt like Dorothy in Oz when she realized that all she has to do to get what she wanted was to click together her ruby slippers, or in my case a pair of scuffed up clogs. The girls said in unison, "Mom, it's great!" "And you're going to show everyone what a fine artist you are," added Grace.

I was soon juried into an open studio program, ARTrails, and painted like crazy to have enough work for the two weekends of visitors. I prepared emotionally, too. I'd heard it's not easy to host hundreds of people in your personal painting space. I still had to install a wood stove and get my painting sink connected. My picture was in the paper, in my fake studio in our bedroom, taken in anticipation of the real deal. Wow, it's happening! I'm doing it and I'm as ready for ARTrails as I'll ever be, I told myself.

Dad directed cars into parking slots behind my old studio, the garage. Two large groups had arrived at the same time. They followed the path to my studio, which was tucked into redwoods and above a little creek. The interior looked new, with none of the customary paint splotches, and some guests commented on it. But I could tell that they were charmed by

the art space. Then a few more people came in. Soon the studio was full. I felt hopeful and edgy at the same time.

"Boy, I'd sure like to see the mind that created all this," a man whispered to me.

"Uh, I'm that mind," I said

"Oh, I don't get some of the titles, like that 'Waiting for Eggplant' one over there."

The painting was large. It featured an aubergine-colored woman wearing a big hat sitting in the style of Donald Duck's nephews, Huey, Dewey, and Louie, fork and knife at the ready.

"Well she's the color of eggplant," I lamely explained. "And she's got her knife and fork in hand. She's waiting for eggplant, waiting for her dinner, what she's ordered at the café."

"Well, I'm still not sure I get it, but good imagination," he said and went off to find his party of art-goers. I saw that this would be a long weekend trying to explain what it is I do.

Narrative painters aren't understood. We're often asked to explain our storied paintings. Maybe it'd be best to just ask the viewer, "Well, what story do you see in the piece?"

I'll never find a good way to explain why in my art world, deer sip cocktails and people fly. Magic happens, and there are shape shifters everywhere. I learned to mention Chagall—how he taught me that painters can ignore the laws of gravity. Frida Kahlo painted her pieces intense and very personal. Matisse used simplified patterns and shapes that made me feel that I could be an artist.

In the past I made puppets and art dolls, sewed clothing, painted on boxes, benches and scarves. I've suffered and smiled through many art openings, and with this open studio event, I came out of the art closet to declare myself an artist. Just that label alone had taken years. A badge of courage and foolishness.

Oh, and that 'Waiting for Eggplant' piece? It went off to the waiting room of a big law office in San Francisco. The clients wait for the lawyers as she waits for her eggplant.

Conversation

The deer sips a cocktail with me;
I find we have a lot in common.
I bring some grassy biscuits,
serve him a platter of berries.

The deer tells me all the latest,
all I need to know
to finish his antlers,
to make the girth of his
crossed haunches
match up in space with
his dainty thin ankles,
just above hooves.

One hoof hangs off the sofa,
one is grounded on
the living room floor

It's called art, I tell the deer.

Sipping Cocktails with Deer

I follow a long tradition of studio painting. Sometimes I paint from a still life, sometimes from a model at a figure drawing group like The Donkey Barn Studio, or from a photo. Often I paint from a dream or from my waking imagination. Even if I paint from something right in front of me, I'm still making it fit my concept of reality. I give a chair legs that could never hold it up in the real world, or tilt a head at a preposterous angle. Not quite as out there as Picasso with his chameleon-eyed women and chunky legged horses in his post-cubist period. He couldn't help himself. He just had to get up after that lunch, take the bones from the fish he had eaten and make a print from them, and then more and more prints. It's either a drive or an affliction and I haven't figured out which—maybe a bit of both. I'm not comparing myself to the greats, just acknowledging their influence on me and my art.

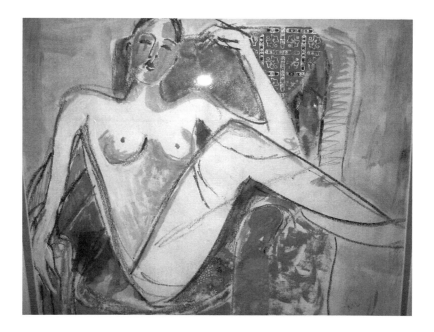

My grandmother first told me I had the hands of an artist when I was seven. All I knew then was that I loved to make things, dishes out of clay dirt in the backyard, tempura paintings of orange groves, one of which won a Los Angeles City Schools prize, and mosaics made from cut up scraps of linoleum left over from Dad's building sites.

When I'm in the studio I want to step out of reality, but at first I feel constrained by the materials I'm working with: a canvas, and some fairly scrubby brushes, acrylic paints, and by all the clutter in the studio. Art papers tucked into baskets, pastel chalks randomly tossed into containers, string, gel medium, pens and pencils, sketchbooks. A huge basket of paints, and brushes in various states of decay. Like me, they all await the arrival of the dreamer's mind.

I like strong and bright colors—ones used by the Fauvists—but today what I've mixed seems muddy. The paint-splattered jar holds disgustingly dirty water. I dump it out and pour in some fresh and while I'm at it, I water the philodendron next to the sink. The plant has to be near water or I'd never think to water it. I'm rarely pragmatic in the studio, except to analyze the dilemma of the painting—how to create the initial composition. What to include, what to toss out. The viewer's eye must move around the piece, and in my case, the elements have to hold together to suggest a story to the viewer.

Now, I'm in a new studio on Fiori Lane; it's smaller and cozy and has soft filtered natural light coming in the bargain windows I picked out. In the fall, my mind turns to the myth of Persephone. The daughter of Demeter, she is lusted after by Lord Hades, who brokers a deal with her father Zeus. Lord Hades captures Persephone and brings her as his bride to the underworld. Demeter, goddess of the harvest, suffers terribly and her grief ruins the harvest and makes the green disappear. Finally, a second deal is made, this time allowing Persephone to return to her mother in the spring and summer, going back to

Hades for fall and winter. The myth is a strong one for mothers of daughters.

Personally, I resist the charms and beauty of autumn. It's hard for me to let go of warmth, sunshine, and the fecund seasons. I imagine Demeter, waiting out the cold for the return of her daughter Persephone. A mother of three daughters, I start to connect emotionally with the piece I work on. My daughters are all married now, and I don't really see them that often. I miss the hubbub of the days when all five kids were home, even if some of them were sharing a spider-filled painting space with me.

This large 4'x5' canvas has held a mermaid, a geisha, and is now becoming Demeter. So far I just have just chalked in her outline and begun to paint the background. But I like her a lot. I don't miss the other women who are now buried below her, like in an Egyptian tomb, or like the phantom paintings museum art restorers look for under old masterpieces. Apparently even the masters didn't always like what they painted the first time, and maybe they threw down their egg

tempera paint, their oils and brushes and asked themselves if they would ever learn to paint. I can just see the edges of a fan shape from the geisha era and I wonder if anyone else will notice this echo of the destroyed image.

I mix paint for the face, neck, and arms of Persephone's mother, Demeter. I use my painting table as a quick palette, brown Kraft paper taking on an art palette life. Now that the body is blocked in, I return to the background and apply layers and layers of paint. Luckily I'm ambidextrous, so I switch hands when one gets tired. And I'm switching brushes as well, different sizes, different tips for the details versus plain background. I stop and take a good look. Wow, I think, I have a long way to go. It's always easy to discount progress.

I take a break and go down to the house to make some lunch. I can't go back to Demeter when I return to the studio, so I pull out a different piece, put it on the easel, adjust all the knobs and screws, to tighten the painting into my grip. Now it can't wiggle away from me, or suddenly slam to the floor, face down.

I sometimes call my friend Diane for help when I'm stuck. She arrives and I show her the piece that is morphing into Persephone's mother and she likes it. But then we move to the problem piece. The piece contains images: a bird, a flying heart, a knight chess piece, a chessboard and swirling comet shapes. Everything looks equal. Nothing really grabs the viewer's attention. Separate blobs on the canvas.

"Make the horse bigger. It should be your focus. Put the bird over to the right and up higher," she says scratching out the bird with the dark chalk, and adding a basic bird shape above with the light pastel. "Hey, did you know a flying heart is an old Sufi symbol."

"No," I say, "but that makes me like it even more."

Diane and I laugh and chat as we walk to the house for a cup of tea and a scone.

After she goes, I return to the studio and proceed to wipe off Demeter's chalk lines with the sleeve edge of my paint

sweatshirt—what used to be my best sweatshirt—until I wore it into the studio. Now the whole right-hand side of the shirt is multi-colored from where I've wiped my brushes—a quick way to remove excess paint.

I begin to paint over large swirling comets with what artists call white-out, a combination of titanium white and whatever is left on the palette. I replace them with small circles, a five-pointed star in the center of each circle. Originally symbols for goddess worshipers, they were later turned into something that stands for the devil: patrimony, pentagrams, five pointed stars. I like this symbolism, but mainly I just like the way they look.

So far the background has been purple, light green and now light blue. I bring the painting down to the house to show

Forrest who says, "It should all be lighter and more distinct in color and contrast." What does he know? He's a computer programmer. But, often he's right about these things.

I walk back down to the studio. It's late, and on this autumn afternoon, getting dark early. I turn on the studio lights and sling the painting back on the paint-encrusted easel, with paint so thick on the bottom tray that I have to turn the paintings sideways now, to complete the very bottom. I toss out the paint water again and fill the jar with clean water.

Painters either treat their paintings like precious babies, or they handle them much like I do, slinging them, taping up small tears with duct tape, and thickly over-painting them. We strive to be alpha dogs of painting so that the success, sometimes elation, or sheer humiliation is ours. That's part of being an artist, along with the materials, the slop of the paint jars, the used-up brushes, the small scraps of paper all over the floor. And coming up with new ideas from nothing. That's what it's about, not always, as people often assume, "playing out in the studio all day." I'm glad no one is around to hear me swearing and fretting or to see me dancing around to African music, paint flinging from the brush.

The next day I work all morning to finish the chess piece, putting a green sprig in the bird's beak, and adding a complimentary colored yellow-red-orange outline around the blue chess piece. A turquoise shade now, something between a phallo blue and a light cobalt blue. The flying heart remains pretty much the same as it was. I'm pleased with the result and know from experience I'd better stop now. Although the temptation is to keep going, it can lead to an overworked piece, a dud. There's a point at which the painter has to call it quits and call the painting finished and I decide, according to my gut reaction, this is it. I hear an owl in the tree outside the studio and realize I need to finish up, it's getting late. It's dark, and long past dinner time. Still, I can't go down yet. I'm not through.

I get out the Noah's Ark animal book that my sister Diane has given me and intently study deer, their chiseled faces and rounded bodies. I close the book and pull out a canvas that has a red pot painted in on one side, and sketch in a deer's face on the other side. I can't resist giving the deer rather human eyes, with soft long eyelashes, something I think deer actually have. The deer now feels like a long-lost relative newly discovered on the Internet. I'm happy with the deer. I feel I know the deer, am intimate with the deer.

I follow an urge and paint apple blossoms on the deer's antlers, the blossoms I would see from the studio windows if it were spring. I push the limits here between whimsy and too cute and I worry about people's reactions. I sit on the tall studio stool to think. I'm out of ideas. Where's the muse? The inner critique has driven the dreamer away for the night.

It's been years since that first studio at the dormitory house, and I have several years of open studios under my artist's beret now. I know that everyone who looks at a piece will see something completely different. One viewer will think the cactus pot with deer painting soft and lovely, another will see the prickles carved into the contrasting paint of the moon behind. One might ask, "Why the moon, why the cactus, and would a deer live in the same place as a cactus?" Yet another will suggest, "Take the blossoms off the antlers, for god's sake." A woman might cry and say it reminds her of her divorce and how she identifies with the deer, just beginning to blossom. And a studio visitor will tell me that they worship small deer somewhere in Latin America where the cactus grows profusely. I'm always amazed, but these diverse stories make me feel the piece is a success.

I count my blessings. Some people don't even have a place to call home. But, for now, for me, the days of sharing space with black widow spiders and the planned War Hammer battles in the garage are over. I have a separate little space, all my own just to make the messes required for art.

This second studio, a transformed old building with an add on, was very inexpensive to create, with recycled windows and doors. I've glazed all the walls to make it cheery and kind of old European. I've spent messy hours with a sponge, a brush and a rag to get this effect. Two of my grandchildren have helped glaze the walls, adding their hand prints. I've taught them how to look at something and find a way into a painting. They surprise me one day with handmade bird nests, mud made from dirt they've dumped into the fountain outside. They use grass and string to help hold the mud nests together. I'm a little miffed when I have to empty the fountain and clean it out, but I have to admire their ingenuity.

Another grandson makes a complete nest around a table by weaving the whole thing with pine tree branches and pine needles. He leaves a square shaped opening as his nest door.

These kids have learned their lessons well. I think one day they may chat with deer, see apple blossoms on its antlers.

Bats in the Belfry

For about two years, in the middle of the night when I had insomnia, I'd get up from the cozy bed to pour a glass of port and sit on the love-seat reading a book. Many of these nights I heard scratching and chewing above me inside our walls, but I decided to take the denial path. Maybe it was just more field mice who'd found their way in through any number of routes in our 50-year-old house.

For these same years my husband asked, when he came in the front door after work, "Do you smell a kind of earthy smell?" I actually joked many times, "You mean that bat guano scent—ha ha." A part of me knew. Later a bat guy described it as a "rustic odor" and told me it was really the bat urine, not the guano that caused a "sort of damp earth smell."

The first glimpse of the bats in the belfry happened in early summer at about five in the evening one month before the bat professionals came into our lives. I heard that scratching noise and ran outside to see if I could pinpoint where the noise was coming from. In the screened air vent tucked under the eaves, I saw a place where the screen was flapping as a bony foot, kind of mouse-like, kicked out mice pellet-like poops, that looked uncannily like sprinkles I've used to decorate the top of cupcakes. There was a pile of them on the ground directly below the vent.

I held my breath. I thought I saw rodent-like ears, but there was something that looked like a bird wing. My heart sank. "Bats!" I whispered out loud. Something so shameful about bats in the belfry meaning crazy and memorialized in books and recent songs by reggae bands, and even by local gravelly voiced Tom Waits. Bats in the belfry, the bell tower, a saying from the 20th century and not as you'd think from old English times.

Hosting bats seemed shameful—-like not paying attention, like when the kids first got lice, or fleas got into the carpet from our cats and only when there were too many to ignore did I shift into action mode with the flea bombs and the lice treatments for the whole family.

I called an exterminator who arrived the next day. He simply looked at the poop and said, "Oh that's guano, you've got bats." He proceeded to climb a ladder and shine a flashlight into the vent. "Yes, cute little fellers sound asleep in there. Well, I can't handle this; we're forbidden to exterminate bats, they're protected and must be humanely released after dark. After they fly out for the evening's mosquito hunt, nail up a screen to keep them from coming back."

My neighbor Mike found out about the bats and insisted on releasing them from the attic. To him bats are varmints and varmints need to be removed as quickly as possible. It was still light out when he climbed the ladder and ripped off the screen. What seemed like dozens of very small bats whipped past us, practically knocking Mike from the ladder. "Wow," we say at the same time. Then I hand him the lavender scented "bat repellent," and he tosses it in the hole. I cut some gopher wire to size and hand it to Mike who screw guns it into place. Mission accomplished, as George W. Bush said.

Friends told me things could be worse than bats in the attic because, after all, bats are good, they eat bugs. And I heard lots and lots of jokes about bats in the belfry—a nice way to call someone kind of crazy, kind of batty. Bats often live in chimneys, hop kiln towers, attics, or church bell towers. Or in my case, in two of the four houses I lived in at the West Pole. Bats are affiliated with the dark side, with dark magic and therefore, witches—not ones from Wiccan clan.

Bats are mammals, even the grandkids know this.

"Mammals have hair, or fur. Grandpa, even though you're bald, you're still a mammal," said Diri, age six, when we had one of many discussions about bats. I thought of bats as a kind of a crazy combination of a bird and a rodent, not at all as mammals, not like us. Not giving live birth and breast feeding their young. For me, vampires came to mind. Bats, with their needle sharp teeth and black cloaks floating out behind. but once I knew our attic was home sweet home to dozens of bats, and bat babies, known as "pups," I wanted to know all about these uninvited house guests. I spent hours on the Internet reading about them. It didn't really make me like them any more than before. I didn't really care about the bat rescue sites. I found that a woman from Sonoma County, Pat North, a big proponent of bats, had just died. She had them as pets and took them into schools to show children just how sweet and charming they really are. The message on the Bat Conservancy phone suggested that, "Maybe Pat is now darting around in bat heaven." I was not happy Pat had died, I just couldn't relate to her love of the bat.

For nights after the exterminator explained that we have bats, not rats in our attic, I couldn't sleep. After the adult bats were maybe not so kindly forced to leave their roost, the bat guy who was hired to deal with the remnants of bat life upstairs—guano, urine laden insulation and possible disease microbes—told me that when he was up in the crawl space evaluating the work entailed for the clean up, that he "didn't feel alone." He had company up there—"Bats, not too many, hanging from the rafters," he said. "More bat removal is needed before we can get to the other. We will need to come back with a bat screen."

A bat screen, he explained, is a long piece of dark heavy plastic. He said that it would act as a one way ticket to the forest behind us, or into, we hoped, the brand new bat house purchased at our local Sebastopol Hardware store.

Because the bats' spiny wings barely support their body weight when they fly out of our attic through a convenient hole in an air vent, they first have to do a kind of free fall and then whoosh upward, settling into a classic dodge, dart and swoop flight pattern chasing after mosquitoes. And bats love mosquitoes; they gobble them up by the thousands. With our various fountains and water gardens about, I had always marveled at our lack of mosquitoes. When the bats returned from their feast, they'd use sonar to find their way back in, straight on into the hole. The one way screen allowed for the free fall drop, but not the straight ahead flight back home to the roost. Even though I went outside to look for bats leaving every night at dark, I saw nothing. But I didn't hear scratching any more, just an occasional flutter.

As we get into the release of the bats their babies, their "pups," are dying up there. Their parents cannot fly back through the "bat screen" that's been installed.

"The pups just won't make it," I'm told. We've picked roosting season to escort our bats back out to the wild. I cried in bed thinking of the abandoned pups, dehydrating and no bat mom and dad. No baby bat milk for the pups.

The bat man has told me bats are clever and persistent and they find their way back home. In this case, ours. Before this bat man came to visit our house, the only other bat man was our grandson Bubby, who was in love with Bat Man and then Spider Man. All the screened vents, some of which also had holes, needed to be replaced.

Finally the clean up is completed: Soiled insulation removed, attic crawl space Hepa vacuumed by a guy wearing a respirator. He had to protect himself because, he explained, bat guano can cause histoplasmosis and other lung diseases, even here in California. (And me with lifelong asthma!) And there is always the possibility of rabies, but that required a bite. I'm told that the bite of these small Northern California bats didn't even hurt. "Their teeth are so small and so sharp, it's not even as bad as getting a tattoo," the tatted-out batman said. His boss came to inspect, "Looks good, no more bats or signs of bat life. Looks like they've been out for at least a week. What our guy found was only crisped babies and a few adults."

Ugh, that made me feel terrible, but at the same time, I'm happy. No more thoughts of bats dangling upside down waiting for nightfall, even if it's something as inane and possibly good, as going after mosquitoes.

I still don't have a lot of mosquitoes and don't see bats swarming after dark. Then I found one screen that had not been replaced. It had a small hole.

Snake Creeps Down

I can't quite get the eagle's beak part of *single whip*; my hand starts to cramp as it becomes the beak. Tonight I'm right behind Forrest, so I try harder than usual to do everything correctly, constantly checking my *core channel*, the line that runs through the top of the head, with roots to heaven and earth. Tai chi is not just in one direction and he'll soon be behind me, able to see how I'm too straight and not bending forward enough in *brush knee*. Later, at home, he may show me how the moves are really supposed to be done. He's only trying to help me, he'll say. Like all the studying he does, he pays close attention and gives it 100%.

We started tai chi to decrease our stress levels, and to do a form of moving meditation. Also, we thought it would be good to do something together; our lives now run in such separate directions.

I always thought the graceful slow moves of tai chi a kind of Asian ballet, so I was shocked when I first learned that the studied, flowing moves—*repulse monkey, carry tiger to mountain, fair lady works the shuttles*—can actually break arms or throw an opponent to the ground when done swiftly and with force. Tai chi is all about keeping your balance and knowing you have the means to defend yourself if needed. It is a martial art; it just looks like dance.

Forrest does tai chi three times a week. An ordered sort of man, my husband is persistent and methodical, a mathematician. I, on the other hand, am an artist with a mind full of cartoon images and wandering, inconsistent thoughts. During *slow set* I imagine myself a woman warrior as I swoop low, right arm and hand pointing down to the floor, *needle to bottom of the sea.* I'm not quite low enough, and when I come out into the *heel kicks,* my leg seems too straight and not high enough. I'm lucky to make it through the hour and a half Monday night class. Once a week is all I can do. I've done it for nine years.

In the middle of summer and in winter, Forrest goes to tai chi camp. I don't want to pay for torture, for hours of *white crane* and *high pat on horse* and sleep in a bunk bed. But I show up for the one evening of *slow set* and follow along, staying afterward for dinner and then skits filled with tai chi related puns and songs. It reminds me of long-ago summers, of inventing new words for old camp songs, and laughing with sticky chocolaty s'mores smeared all over my face.

I'm always a little jealous when my husband leaves for camp, knowing he'll be doing the kicks and bends, sweating, and slowly bowing to strange and beautiful women from all over the country, even though our house, with me in it, is three miles down the road. Camp is on the hilly grounds of a local church campsite. There's a swimming pool and small cabins tucked into redwood groves. When the weather is nice, students do classes on the grass outside. Nighttime classes and dinner are in the big high-ceilinged hall with smooth wooden floors. The meals are vegetarian and the parties and dancing go on into the dark.

Once, a few years ago right after camp was over, Forrest called to say he was coming home with our friend, Don, and a woman named Star (that was really her name) whom he had met at camp. He said he thought I'd like Star and that we had "a lot in common." He explained she was from Los Angeles and was an artist.

When they showed up I saw that what he left out of the description was that she was beautiful, youngish and tall with a long thick mane of blonde hair. "She's a tai chi goddess," he said to me over the phone, and as she relaxed outside in my garden talking to Forrest and Don while I finished making dinner, I understood only too well that she was also a plain ordinary goddess.

I can still remember our little group eating outside on the picnic table together. I'm trying to be gracious. I smile a lot, but imagine myself crouching into *strike, parry, punch,* and *parting the wild horse's mane* and flinging my opponent to the floor.

I have trouble with the green thing. For me, jealousy's an emotion that easily jumps to the surface, bowing low and then driving home a direct body blow that takes me down. But when Star gets ready to leave, we hug, and I decide that she can't help it if she was born to be a goddess. I look at my husband and he gives me one of his winks. It's conspiratorial, and suggests, "I know what you're thinking— you'd better just forget it."

Jane, our teacher, is small, compact and low to the ground. She's built for tai chi. Knees bent, she demonstrates some of the more difficult moves, and then we students copy her form, except it doesn't look the same. "Lower your center of gravity, concentrate on the *dantien*." Easy for her to say when she is so much lower already, with her center of gravity, her belly button closely rooted down into the gym floor of Salmon Creek School, with the salmon trying to spawn nearby. They leap up the rocks, water pounding down on them as we push against earth's gravity and try to strike poses of animals, birds, reptiles.

I've known Jane since she first moved here with her musician boyfriend over thirty years ago. She was studying the Yang form in San Francisco with her Chinese tai chi master. That was before she became a teacher with her own following. "The Cult of Jane," is what I call it. Her devoted students cling to her words, eager to experience every correction, and bring offerings of fruit and veggies from their gardens, eggs from their chickens, and other tokens of appreciation. They carefully *step back to ride tiger*. She sells tee shirts imprinted with her image or small sculptures of her with fans doing a fan set move, foot in the air. Her website is a twist on her name, Golden Jane.

When Jane shares pictures taken at camp, Forrest selects a few and brings them home, leaving them out on the table for me to look at later. As I drink my morning tea, I pick up the photos. In one Forrest does *push hands* with a woman and both of them are laughing. It looks like a crush to me, a fling, an affair, a love match. Some sort of ugly Chinese serpent began to wind its way into the pit of my stomach, *snake creeps down*.

I turn a lovely shade of celadon. I've been bitten by the snake, and it seems reasonable when I reflect on my history with men. They have looked at me with their serpent's eyes and told me lies as smoothly as reptiles glide through the tall rattle snake grasses around here. A flying jumble of thoughts practically kick me over.

I hope my green has turned to just a mere hint of jaundice when Forrest arrives home from work. I casually grasp the photo in my hand and say, "Looks like you're having just a little too much fun with this woman. Who is she?" He takes the photo and laughs. This makes me even hotter. Strike! my brain says, the serpent leaning forward, head up and ready, *serpent strikes*.

"You mean you really don't know who this is?"

"No. Who is she?" I ask, a little more harshly than I intend.

"It's us. It's you," he says. "Remember when you came to camp for *slow set* and we did *push hands* after?" Push hands, a circular move is about balance, about defending yourself without falling over or hitting the other, with wrists held just so, the feet and steps precise. The serpent slithers away.

He hands me the photo, still laughing. "Look," he says, "can't you see yourself?"

I look carefully again at the woman. Oh yes, it's me in a photogenic moment. In a moment that captures how much I really enjoy being with my husband, even if we are trying to push each other over. I want to laugh at myself for my foolishness, and from a sense of relief, but I can't laugh. I'm too disturbed by my gross misjudgment and I feel ashamed.

"Hey, you want some of Fern's great Redwood Chai?" Forrest asks. "She gave everyone some tea to take home. Let's have some spicy chai and then watch the old movie I ordered on Netflix." Graceful Fern. Fern of the perfect form, each move liquid, smooth, hypnotic. For a moment I feel the serpent's tail flicker, but then he slithers away to his dark hiding place.

I take the cup of fragrant steaming tea from my husband's hand, sit down on our love-seat.

Next class I get the beak right, my hand doesn't even hurt, and I kick extra high, even though my thigh muscles feel the jolt. This time I'm behind a handsome new man with perfect style. During *golden cockerel stands on one leg* his calf muscles pump out. He's from China and does push hands so skillfully that it takes all of my concentration to stay on my feet as he circles around and around, his wrist against mine.

Maybe I'll start coming to class twice a week. I always go half way with things, and I want to be different. I want to take tai chi seriously. I want to be a tai chi goddess, of sorts.

As we finish the set, my hands relaxed at my sides, standing straight, knees finally unbent, I feel the chi energy flowing through my body, filling up the dark crevices, washing out nasty green serpents. After the tedium of meditative, repetitious moves with dreamy names, we reward each other with bowing and clapping all around. As we clap, I think of that picture of the happy couple who can smile at each other while trying to knock each other off balance. We walk out to our car. The night is a rare balmy one. As Forrest and I drive up the winding hilly road to our home, I sit quietly. I feel a sense of peace, just the way I felt tonight doing *hands like clouds*, like how I felt watching Jane lead fan set, red and black fans rhythmically snapping open and closed.

Make a Fence in the Morning

Gravity binds us together
our limbs
entwine in
fields of heather.

Pale orchards gleam
in mid-day sun
the soldered seams
have come undone.

Make a fence
in the morning
to hold in the love
open the gate

for the mourning dove.

Good Fences Make Good Neighbors

I'm thinking about the Christo Fence again some 37 years after I first saw it, not only because its history is almost as old as my move to Sonoma County, but because a recent viewing of a Running Fence documentary at the Union Hotel in Occidental brought it back to mind.

In 1976, Scott and I had been looking for property to buy in Sonoma County, driving our usual backroads route through Marin County. We'd read in the *San Francisco Chronicle* about an art fence, and we were hoping to see it. Still, as we rounded a curve on Highway 1, we were not prepared for the grandiosity of the fence—the sheer majesty of it as coastal winds wafted rectangular white nylon panels into the air. My mind swirled with metaphors trying to capture what I saw, to turn the sight into the familiar. The fence looked like a fleet of schooners sailing across the hills, or a flock of huge doves, wings soaring.

The tall white fence towered above the roof of our camper, came right up to us and then stopped, only to start up on the other side of the roadway, over and up, until the undulating Christo Fence danced over the distant horizon line. Scott had pulled the VW camper over so all of us could have a longer look at it—so we could comprehend what we all found amazing.

"What exactly does it do?" asked my more pragmatic ten-year-old daughter Grace after a minute of silence.

"It's art," I replied. "It doesn't have to do anything."

"Art and pretty," five-year-old Mary Lea said.

"And very WOW," Scott added.

I agreed. The fence was so much more than I imagined: It impacted the landscape and saluted it at the same time. I knew I would never forget it.

For the documentary showing, the entire Bocce Ballroom, with it's long low-lit interior, the rogue's gallery of Italian ancestors hanging on the walls at the heart of the Union Hotel, is packed to the brim. We're told we can't get in, but Barbara Pozzi Gonella, one of the owners lets the four of us locals sneak in, and fortunately we find seats. It's a standing-room-only event with ranchers and farmers and old hippies and the rest of us. The movie represents an emotional moment, that turning point in the area's history in the 1970s so fraught with troubles between lifestyles. The fence project unintentionally brought all factions of the area together.

Before the film begins, many from the audience get up to share their memories and all say how they grew to love the short-lived white fence and its creators, Jeanne Claude and her husband, internationally famous artist, Christo. Mostly the speakers are sons and daughters of the ranchers who allowed access so that the fence could cross over 59 properties in Marin and Sonoma Counties and then end up in the Pacific Ocean. They talk with humor and a definite pride that they were a piece of this historical event. Without them, it wouldn't have happened.

Our hostess, Barbara Pozzi Gonella, shares a memory too. She explains that when her dad, Portuguese cattle rancher Ed Pozzi, first met Jeanne Claude and Christo, he thought them, "hippies looking for work repairing fences."

"He told them," Barbara recalls, "we have plenty of help from our kids with repairing fences." But the charismatic red-haired French Jeanne Claude and her Bulgarian husband returned several more times to finally sell the concept to Pozzi and to secure his cooperation. Once this happened they had an in with all the other ranchers and farmers.

My metal folding chair is a little uncomfortable, but the black and white documentary soon takes my mind off my discomfort and transports me into the story.

It begins with a panorama of the area the fence traveled and then focuses on Valley Ford, the only town the fence would cross, and which required an Environmental Impact Report. The film shows how important the Post Master in tiny block-long Valley Ford became to the success of the art project. He spread the word and shared Christo's amazing fence sketches at the post office. He helped people understand the scope, and how the couple had done similarly challenging art projects in nature before.

Next the film shows the amazingly detailed drawings Christo made to show what the fence would be made of, and how it would look. Soon, to the property owners, the farmers and ranchers of the area, the couple became known as, "the guy from the Iron Curtain and his French wife." Their charisma and charm bring them to the tables of these ranch families. There are a delightful set of photographs of them eating dinner together with families of four, six, nine at simple sturdy farm tables. The couple got to know the kids and the ranch animals, their way of life. The documentary shows it, and the relatives of the ranchers at this sold-out viewing, confirm it. Some of the little kids pictured in the film are now in their forties and fifties and their hair is gray.

I find it fascinating that Christo and Jeanne Claude took all these people into their artistic net that stretches around the globe and turned this fence into life-long friendships across cultures, and continents, across such different backgrounds with the powerful language of conceptual art. The ranchers and farmers came to the county hearing in full support of Christo's fence. With the help of Christo's consulting engineers and hundreds of volunteer laborers, a magical fence was born.

I feel kind of sad seeing pictures of the young Jeanne Claude, charming front woman for the long-married couples' works. I know that she died of an aneurysm two years ago when she was 72. I'm close to that age; it seems too young to die. All the local artists I know mourn her passing. She was dynamic and driven by a strong and passionate inner vision. To us she represents the courage, and the persistence of a great conceptual artist. She didn't have formal art training, but her eye was excellent and her imagination unbelievably large. I met her once and she exuded style and warmth. She and her husband Christo, like Patti Smith and Robert Mapplethorpe in Patti Smith's *Just Kids,* were sure of their intent. After the fence project, they went on to wrap iconic buildings in cloth, create an ochre cloth gateway in Central Park and plant giant umbrellas to shimmer in the California sunshine. The scale of what this couple, who always worked as a team, attempted and completed, was notoriously grand in scale, and their ability to convince the doubters, amazingly successful. I feel a pang of envy and a sense of dismay at my own lack of confidence, lack of thinking big. Even though I have finally established myself as an artist, I am always questioning the value of what I create, the impact, if any, of what I make, what I imagine.

They never looked back or questioned their wild ideas. In the case of the running fence, the idea was to intersect nature with man-made art so that each enhanced the other. The Christo fence stood for just two weeks, after four years in the planning, and 400 paid laborers pounding stakes into the fertile ground. The film shows tiny people clinging like lead fishing weights, to the bottoms of the nylon sails as they tried to tackle them into the hoops and loops, and hook them into metal poles.

Maybe the ranchers felt a little like farmer Yasgur did about Woodstock—proud to have been a part of a historical event, but still scratching their heads about exactly what it all meant.

I wonder how Christo will go forward without Jeanne Claude by his side. I wonder why I can't be more like them. More convinced, more daring in my art.

I met a woman from nearby Valley Ford at Whole Foods a few days ago. She's lived here even longer than I have, but isn't a native either. I asked her if she was around for the building of the fence.

"I fell in love with it, and had to go look at it every day—in fog, and in sun, on a windy cloudless day. All days were spectacular!" she said smiling.

Another woman and I struck up a conversation at the gym. I knew her from when I first moved to Occidental. I asked her if she remembered the Christo Fence.

"Remember it? I worked on it daily until we finished hooking up all the panels to the poles." She glowed with pride and flashed me a great big smile. "It was one of the hardest but most satisfying times of my life."

And what about the remnants? By agreement the fence had to be completely dismantled after two weeks and all materials, the 18' high poles, once used in Vietnam, the 24.5 miles of nylon panels and the 350,000 metal hooks were left with the ranchers. For years I've seen these panels, danced or picnicked under them, seen people bid on them at auctions. We used a panel to cover the stage for a country fashion show that my partner and I cooked up to help our little fabric store. The sun lit up the cloud-like panel until it practically glowed.

The farmers cut up the metal and expanded their own ranch fences. Sheep and cattle grazing near pieces of history. Bits of the Running Fence remain behind—the practical application of an amazing art project. The film shows all this.

Farmers, ranchers, hippies, Italians, Portuguese dairy herders, their families and this eccentric couple marked, for all time, the hills and valleys between Petaluma, Valley Ford and the sea. It wove together Marin and Sonoma Counties. Wove them, like a white woolen coat, turned them into flocks of fluttering doves, or maybe what we saw were a thousand sails of a thousand ships. My mind, after all these years, still grabs at a way to describe it. What I do know is that I'll always remember the sight, never lose the emotional impact it had on me, and how it proved to everyone who helped, who let it pass across their land, or like me, those who saw it, that good fences truly do make good neighbors.

Quan Yin: Goddess of Mercy and Compassion

It's moving day for Quan Yin, my little spiritual companion at this house on Fiori Lane. She's watched over weddings and celebrations. She's seen soccer balls fly toward her, sticks tossed for the dog lobbed in her direction. She's heard me sing, whistle and cry in our back garden. The gardens here are fertile; Luther Burbank had it right—Sonoma County is the "Chosen spot as far as all of nature is concerned." Plants thrive—become almost a jungle. Small Quan Yin slowly disappears into foliage.

Her bare toes are down there in the dirt, in soft gopher mounds. She's tucked into aromatic rose geranium leaves. The swirls of Quan Yin's soft carved sienna skirt lie buried in rose blossoms and thorns, hidden by lavenders and vines.

The weathered folds of her fabric are a nesting place for mud wasps. The wasps have cleverly deposited bits of mud mixed with their saliva into the cavities, and when I water, I notice their larvae wriggling in her skirt. Hummingbirds buzz over her head to get at nearby nectar, flying right past her third eye, the bindi in the middle of her terra cotta forehead. I worry that as she disappears so will my commitment to forgiveness. There's a lot to forgive in life, starting with oneself.

It's been a while since Forrest helped me put this statue of Quan Yin into a place of honor in the garden, just before my daughter Mary Lea's outdoor wedding in September, 2000. For me, Quan Yin is a requirement for any marriage celebration and I wanted her here as a witness to my daughter and her husband's vows. I needed my own reminder to forgive, even if I can't ever forget. When I see Quan Yin's sheathed sword I understand that compassion doesn't come easy; sometimes it's a battle.

The goddess of compassion and mercy was once a man. Quan Yin has undergone a sex change during her lifetime and come out the other side a more understanding deity. She always knew she was a man in goddess's clothing. Originally an Indian God, Avalo Kitesvara, Quan Yin traveled along the Silk Roads. As he traveled he slowly became a mustachioed woman, transforming into Kuan Shih Yin, "the one who hears the cries of the world, the expression of loving compassion." In those times before men were able to hold the feminine aspects of themselves equal to the male, he had to become a she—the yin and the yang not yet one lovely perfect circle.

I think the sex change had to do with the lush flow of yards of smooth soft silk—smuggled from country to country along mountain routes. The touch of silk on my skin, makes me feel more feminine. I guess that's why it's in my lingerie drawer and why I pick it for that special outfit when I want to be a softer woman.

On September 11, 2001, my daughter Grace called. She was watching TV news, something I haven't done for over 25 years; the suffering aspects of the daily newscast are way too much for me. "You always said if anything important happens in the world somehow you'll hear about it, so I thought you'd want to know."

She said, "Planes are crashing into buildings and all planes have been grounded. Some are missing, They think some are headed for California. Pay attention, Mom, go up to your studio and listen to your radio."

So I did what she said. I stayed in the studio that day and the next several days and listened and painted. First I worked on a fallen disembodied head, like a stone relic with a look of shock on its face. I kept on painting, adding a fiery Phoenix-looking bird nesting on the head. I thought about a title, and decided I would call it *Discovery*. I started on a second painting, a big, buxom angel with short hair holding a round blue pot with a fully bloomed white rose. Her eyes closed, her composure sad. Her title: *Compassion*.

I knew the men without a feminine side would want to go bomb and burn—an eye-for-an-eye, tooth-for-a-tooth retribution. More innocents, children and families would die; the price for the lost Americans. I sat near small Quan Yin's feet. "Help me understand," I ask. "Mercy and Compassion," I repeated.

We joined hundreds of thousands of others in San Francisco to protest a possible invasion of Iraq. We stood in Occidental with a handful of others on the Bohemian Highway holding candles in the night air and giving the peace sign to the few cars passing by. All to no avail.

In October 2001, a month after 9-11 happened, I opened my studio to the public for ARTrails. I hoped for a lot of visitors.

I cleared the decks, placed round clear glass pebbles on the windowsills, put abundant bouquets of white flowers around, and even got down on the floor and stenciled white doves onto the wood. I'd toned down the wild, colorful atmosphere of my studio and paintings. I wanted the studio to convey peace and love. Our mantra of the 1960's. My center piece was *Compassion,* and next to her, *Discovery*, the painting I'd done while hearing about people holding hands and jumping from rooftops in New York.

As visitors arrived and walked from their cars to the studio, I played a tape a friend brought me, the Buddhist nuns chanting over and over again, "May all the animals, all the humans, all sentient beings be free from suffering." Sacred painting space—thoughts of compassion and mercy. I needed to hear the words myself, a boost to get through two challenging week ends.

Some people saw the *Discovery* piece as quirky, a funny Harry Potter character with a bird hat; a few saw her as a relic; a very few really got what I intended; nobody got what I felt as I painted her, waiting to see if the Golden Gate Bridge might be blown up. *Discovery* sold during Open Studios to a Santa Rosa ad agency for their main wall, but no one bought *Compassion*.

Several months later, the Arts Council had a 9-11 show in Petaluma, the funds to go to New York City. I donated, *Compassion* and she was purchased by a guy I knew from Bodega, an eccentric man who had a large acreage on the edge of the forest where he had horses. I heard he kept most of his art in a bunch of abandoned cars on his property and I worried that *Compassion* would be ruined. I thought it just another example of keeping mercy out of sight.

Some time after this auction, the man who bought *Compassion* died. He was a drinker but they say he died from grief over the death of his two horses, who had eaten a poisonous shrub. At his memorial, sitting on the stage, there was *Compassion,* front and center and looking sharp. My artist friend Betty Ann said she'd been able to scrub off mold, revealing the bright paint below. She surrounded my painting with others from his collection, mainly landscapes by well-known Sonoma County painters. Plein Aire types. There were a few pieces, she said, that just couldn't be salvaged.

After two friends suffered tragedies, I bought a second Quan Yin. I needed even more of my one remnant of spiritual belief, the belief in the importance of mercy, of compassion. I already knew about the whims of fate, but what I wanted to try to control was myself—my reactions to people and events.

A human-sized Quan Yin, she stands outside the studio where I can easily see her from one of the windows. She's by the water garden, a small circular cement pond with plants and goldfish. I placed a small cactus in Studio Quan Yin's upturned palm, and hoped it would survive our West County winters—that year particularly cold with some ferocious windstorms, knocking the power out for four days. Every time I thought for sure the little cactus flower must be dead, I was pleased to find it still alive, sometimes just a different color, my favorite a lovely reddish color with green at the tips.

I'm very fond of my two Quan Yins. They're different, but equally powerful, both with elaborate carving. My grandkids like to climb up the bigger studio Quan Yin and my grand-daughter whispers secrets into Quan Yin's ear.

Little Quan Yin is practically invisible. The meditation garden has grown up around her in the 10 years since that garden wedding. We need to see her so we have to move her and it's a two- person job. Compassion is heavy.

"Just decide exactly where you want it and I will help, but not until then," my husband informs me. So, now I have to decide. Where can we see her, but protect her from wild grandchildren antics?

"I've found the spot," I say a week later.

"Are you very sure?" he asks. He knows my slippery ways. My changeable mind.

"Yes."

We go outside and I prune back roses and honeysuckle so that we can move her without being scratched by thorns or entangled in vines. I've already blasted the wasps with a hose and they seem to have moved on, the mud nests just dusty residue.

We both struggle as we lift her, she's made of real concrete, none of that fake stuff. I have prepared a flat, level spot for her behind a beautiful low metal fence with a jeweled glass center. Made by my friend Marta, who died from brain cancer a few years ago, I think the artwork a perfect complement to her fancy swirls and it will prevent any errant soccer balls from knocking her down or damaging her.

"Looks good, she fits perfectly,my husband says.

"Yes," I say smiling, happy that compassion is protected.

We hold hands in the garden under redwood trees and admire our small Quan Yin, and I drift into thoughts of silk roads.

Blameless Eve

They say Eve is responsible for the troubles of the world.

She joined forces with a snake, and without a fork to her tongue,
simply slipped hers into Adam's ear.

"Try it," she whispered, holding
a round red apple—an offering
on her paradisal palm.

And he took a big bite.

They say that was the end of innocence.

But I hold Eve blameless.

It was the sweet juice of an apple that brought Eden down.

Eve's Neighborhood

I live in Eve's neighborhood, apples everywhere. This time of the year, late September, they are falling. If Eve wanted to, she could just point them out to Adam and let him choose one for himself and escape her fate in Eden. There would be no problem about disobeying Daddy, no portraying the woman as seductress and responsible for the fall of humankind. There would just be a happy man eating another apple in the fall.

Apples hang heavily from the branches. Gravid, apples drop into the rich dark dirt of the apple orchards of western Sonoma County at harvest time. I see my neighbors' apple branches propped up with thin rough wooden sticks to keep them from cracking off. We've already heard the steady chunk, chunk, chunk of apples being tossed into bins, and been slowed down driving behind trucks loaded full with Gravensteins, Granny Smiths and Rome Beauties. The green and red striped Gravensteins are usually the first to ripen, and the red apples the last.

Around the time of Sebastopol's incorporation as a city in 1902, apples supported many families of farmers. But things changed. The railroad that used to go right down the middle of town, "the train on Main," when we first moved here in 1979, was torn out. It had picked up apples and taken them to San Francisco for distribution. The first of many blows to the local apple growers.

Then the apple farmers of Washington state, in a sneaky move to become the dominant apple growers, bought the main storage and apple processing plant in Graton, and promptly closed the plant. It took the local farmers years before they worked out a new co-operative system to store and distribute their apples.

When the apples are left to rot on the ground, too many for even the neighborhood deer, raccoons, foxes and birds, the air is heavy with the scent of vinegar and sugar. The year the main crop manager died, the next guy didn't plan ahead, didn't know when to pick what, so the apples in our neighborhood simply turned to vinegar on the ground instead of in the processing plant. When I took my daily walk, I practically had to hold my nose.

The local Whole Foods gives only a token nod to the Sebastopol apple farmers, everything else apple-related comes from Washington state, or at certain times of the year, from far away New Zealand or Chile. But we still celebrate our fruit with an Apple Blossom Festival in spring, even though there are not nearly as many blossoms as there once were. Later on, in August, there's an Apple Harvest Festival with bands, apple bobbing, pie contests, art shows, countrified crafty booths. A kind of nostalgic throw back.

In 1999, the same year we moved into Eve's neighborhood, my art was chosen for the posters, tee shirts, and ads for the blossom festival. The theme was "Renaissance in Blossom." My image was an old-style court jester, a king's fool, juggling apples that numbered the year. The background was filled with white and pinkish blossoms. The juggler had Christmas wrapping paper collaged into his reddish costume, but I hoped no one would notice. I spent a very warm day signing posters and greeting people at the festival. A short moment of apple glory.

Last July as we rounded a curve in the road, we saw that one apple-farming neighbor had cut down about 20 trees, a whole row. I had a visceral reaction to the sight of branches, browning and withered, heaved up into funeral pyres. An apple tree graveyard, stumps still clinging to the earth. The saddest sight was the piled up dead and browning branches filled with hopeful little red apples, too small and bitter for even birds to enjoy.

"Did you see all those felled apple trees?" I asked Forrest when I got home, "and all the short stumps sticking out of the ground?"

"Maybe they are just removing old trees that don't produce anymore," Forrest suggested. He seemed pretty sure they wouldn't be taking down their acres of trees.

"No," I answered, "they haven't harvested their apples for years. I think it's a way for them to avoid the costs of another harvest time that doesn't bring much profit."

I felt the pain of all the trees. I remembered talking to a woman about this a few years earlier, when the apple trees across from her were sacrificed to the chain saw. She claimed to have heard the "screams and cries of the trees." For me, I just shuddered and drove by the ever-widening swath of destruction as quickly as possible. I knew that next we'd see the stumps being pulled out of the ground with a big tractor. The memory still grabs me in the gut, and I wonder if this is how it is to live with urban blight, or in a bombed-out neighborhood. Of course, on a lesser scale.

I fell in love with trees as a kid and remember spending hours talking with them curled up in their branches, or sitting down below, sketching and chatting. I was lucky. My mom seemed to think it perfectly healthy behavior.

I recently watched a You Tube video with Professor Suzanne Simard explaining that under the earth, through their roots, and through mycorrhizal fungi, trees communicate with each other. They actually try to help each other and send each other energy. I believe we can communicate emotionally with plants. I thought so even before the book *The Secret Life of Plants* came out in 1973. Critics thought the book was bunk, but since then, the authors Peter Tompkins and Christopher Bird have been proven correct in their theories about how plants respond to human communication in a positive, or negative way.

From talking with neighbors on our walk we found out that the orchard is being removed in favor of a vineyard. A common scenario around here; the gnarly fruit trees have been replaced by grapes. We've seen this graveyard scene many times in the days since grapes and vineyards became the dominant theme of our local landscape. Vineyards cover the hills where the roots of apple trees once went down deep, not needing well water like the grapes. Water tables continue to drop as more and more thirsty little grape clusters form on the very managed vines, pruned to conform to a shape that makes them easy to harvest. Watering systems are put in, not only to keep the new young plants growing, but to protect them in a frost. These over-managed vines are nothing like the old vine stock, the old survivors I saw in the Pyrenees of France, coming out of rock outcrops and subsisting off of whatever water their roots could reach. And nothing like the way the Italians grew their grapes in Occidental in the early days. I like wine and I drink local wines, and sometimes I feel like someone that resembles the word traitor.

Gravensteins are best for pies. Everyone says so. Mom's Apple Pie, run by Betty Carr, who came here from Japan in 1953, features the Gravensteins. She started out with just apple pies, but now serves 16 varieties of pies and probably makes more money from her pies than from the sale of their apples. Gravensteins may be delicious in pies, but their shelf life is short, and these are days of distance farming. Still, you can't beat Gravensteins for pies. Mom Betty is right!

The Granny Smiths are tart and green and are some of the last to be picked. My neighbor, Cecile, says this year the apples have a lot of "spots" so she doesn't hold out hope for a good price. Apparently apples don't make my neighbors much money. They all pay the same guy to manage their orchards. He plows, and removes the cover crop, usually yellow oxalis, or mustard, so that more water gets to the trees. He also arranges for the picking and the sale of the apples and tends to the farming details that have gotten too large for the neighbors. In the last five years they've all gone organic and we no longer hear spraying equipment moving up and down the evenly spaced lines of trees in the early fog of morning. The apples may have spots and an occasional worm, but now we all rest a little easier without the poison. The last of the apples lie under the trees and in bins. If rains come early, those apples will be slated for vinegar processing.

On picking days, there are men, mostly from Mexico, out in the orchards, on ladders and down below. They shake the apples off and then pluck the remaining. After harvest they will be back to prune everything for the next season. They clatter up metal ladders and leave neat piles stacked high with thin limbs they've pruned away. Sometimes I take a few stacks of these for fire kindling. They are aromatic and get the bigger firewood going. At the right time, later on in the fall, the piles of branches will be burned, smoking out the neighborhood for a day or two.

I remember workers picking our parents' five acres of lemons in the San Fernando Valley in the 1940s when I was little. Those workers sang and laughed and my sister and I wondered at the words they used. "It's Spanish," our mother told us. "Spanish," we repeated, looking at one another and smiling. Our twin brothers, too little to know what Spanish was, were just being babies in bassinets, but were lulled to sleep by Spanish songs. We thought the language kind of like a secret, an exotic, something very special that we were left out of. Even though we weren't permitted by our parents to go anywhere near the picking, we usually snuck in as close as we could get and "spied on them," listening to their songs, which never let up all day long. These newer modern day workers don't sing. Sometimes they whistle, but usually they simply run and pick and toss, the apples creating the melody as they cascade into big wooden bins.

There are vintage apples too, and some odd apples, that when you slice into them are almost a neon pink: pink pearls. They are crunchy and just amazingly pink. We don't see them in our neighborhood, but they are grown as a specialty apple in Sebastopol. They are especially good in salads for their crunch factor and astounding interior color. A man came by my studio once and said he had picked up a whole box of pink pearls across from Andy's on Highway 116 at Hales Apple Farm, and that he would take them back to Los Angeles to give to friends, who always exclaimed over their beauty and fussed over what they consider to be a very special gift. Ironic that I learned about them from him and not from any natives of Sebastopol.

Redwood trees are the backdrop for orchards. Our neighborhood is particularly sunny because large numbers of redwoods have been logged out in the past, roots pulled to create space for pasture land, and later for apple orchards, cherries and plums. Once this was a dark forest and there are still places just behind our house and away from the orchards, where

picuis of mythical orchard

you can re-enter that soft redwood world, with duff thick under the trees, and barely a sign of blue skies.

Now some say Eve served up a pomegranate, and some say she did nothing at all. Some would say Adam should share equally in the blame of the thing. But that fruit, red and ripe, gave humans the knowledge forbidden them by the Christian version of a Creator. I say it's a sexy story that makes Eve out to be a temptress.

After all, it's just an apple. And as much as I love to pry loose the tart sweet seeds of the pomegranate, or cut a piece off for my grandchildren's enjoyment, I prefer the apple. There is something about making chunky applesauce dusted with cinnamon and nutmeg, or filling a crust with sliced apples, fresh lemon juice over the slices, with currants and dots of butter and sugar that makes me switch my brain over from summer to fall.

Give me an apple tossed into a salad, or even soft in a vegetable stew, or cut up into turkey stuffing. Part of the bounty, of our traditions in Eve's neighborhood. Now as I take my daily walk, I snag a few of the last remaining apples, poke them into my pockets or curl my shirt up around them. Sometimes I don't even wait to get home, but crunch into one, juice sweet, dripping down my chin.

Country Tea

Take your shoes off at the door
keep the duff outside
where it belongs.
There's a place by the window
where you can see
rain driving through the tall trees.

That's the place for a cup of tea.
Leaves swirl, form shapes,
show what's to come.

Smoky oolong finds the place
where desire and fatigue
fall together.

Put your shoes on
when you leave the place.
Zip up your jacket tight.
Prepare for burrs,
and mighty blasts of wind.

Try to act like once you lived in the city.

Maiden's Ecstasy

I'm sipping the most beautiful melon-colored green tea. It's the color of kiwi and honeydew—somewhere between celadon and chartreuse. A blend of gen maicha and green tips, the server brings it in a clear glass teapot and pours some for me into a clear glass cup. It's the perfect complement to my meal, a generous piece of honeycomb served with a fabulous Roquefort cheese, smooth and silky white goat cheeses and seeded garlicky flat breads with crisp honey-flavored apple, strawberries and a dewy melon flared out in a fan shape. As an artist, I appreciate the aesthetic of it all, as well as the flavors.

This is my version of heaven, Samovar, a tea shop with paired food in Yerba Buena Gardens south of Mission in San Francisco.

On a rare overnight trip, I've come to the City with my husband who will spend his day listening to software tips, tricks,

issues and how to debug, while I roam about the City like a lioness ready to pounce on beauty, culture, interesting people and food. I've come with a barking cough, and people eye me a little suspiciously. It's flu session and there's a lot of media focus on the swine flu, but I just have an ordinary case of bronchitis due to a change in the weather and lungs scarred from years of asthma. I think the honey comb and the green tea will be medicinal.

In real life I'm not really a lioness, more a country mouse come to the city. No hay seeds or burrs in my socks today, but I do look a little funny with my leggings, skirt, swirly Ugg look-alikes, fur peeking from the tops, my woven sweater from Ireland and a little cream and tan beret with rosettes. Something like a European bag lady. Or the artist that I am.

A tea canister near me catches my eye. "Maiden's Ecstasy," it says on the label. *Try some of that*, the lioness in me growls. The country mouse says, *Don't ask about it*. But the lioness has won.

"Can you tell me about this Maiden's Ecstasy?" I ask my server.

She's a lovely young woman who has a delicious way with words. Honey practically drips from her lips.

"Earth, with undertones of deep forest," she says, "it's fermented and re-fermented until it tastes like something very, well, very dark and sweetly earthy."

I'm not sure exactly how that would bring a maiden to ecstasy, but she says it was once a dowry tea, like the monkey-plucked varieties. The tea has always been labor intensive and the flavor more on the black side than the green. This meant that the tea was considered more valuable in the days of dowry. In the days of maidens. She smiles and looks straight into my eyes. *Poison apples, yes, I'll take a bite,* I think. *Happy to. Lead me into the forest and I'll fall asleep or duck into a house made of gingerbread and candies, or maybe shack up with some dwarfs.*

But I don't try Maiden's Ecstacy. I just continue to slowly munch on and savor my food. Using hands is just fine here, although I do take the fork to the honey comb. I remind myself I'm far from maidenhood now, and just because all the forest myths come to mind, doesn't mean I'll like the tea. I do like the green tea I've chosen for my meal—it's direct and slightly acidic with no deep undertones of anything. More like me than I like to admit. Maybe my days for mossy earthen teas are gone, but I'm still thinking about ordering some Maiden's Ecstasy online, later, when no one can see the label on the canister, except in my tea cupboard—which is overspilling with everything. Licorice tea, gingers, cinnamon seasonal teas, and the usual standards: Irish breakfast for my sister who drinks it black, chai with lots of honey for Rowan, and peppermint for the grandkids—with honey and rice milk to make it a lovely pearl color—"pearl tea." I have white teas and silver needle teas. Lots of greens and a few random ones left over from other times—PMS tea and women's herbal. I have a jar of lavender and one of dried mint from my own garden, for when it's time to make summer teas. My husband makes fun of me and sometimes gets mad when the teas start bursting over into his coffee side of the cupboard. I have three shelves devoted to tea. Forrest has a half shelf with filter cone, filters and a bag of French Roast whole beans.

Today, I lusciously enjoy my lunch, tea, and people watching at the Samovar. I exchange a little conversation with two very handsome men, probably in their 30's. The one, a rather exotic blend himself, is here from Los Angeles "just for the tea—they don't know good tea down there," and he's purchasing four canisters to take back with him. The other fellow, Eric, works at Samovar and has helped the LA guy sip his way through lots of teas. He tells me he's just recently moved away from this busy museum-laden area out to the Mission district. "More like the country," he says. He knows I'll like this because I have just explained where I come from, redwoods, coastal, nature, animals, quiet and more quiet.

At the end of my meal and before he leaves for the day, Eric brings over something that looks like pink lemonade. "This is not on the menu," he says, "but try it."

It is cold and tastes vaguely of lavender. "What do you think?" "I like it." "Lavender saturated lemon juice" he says, "and then chilled." "Oh, I can make this at home, I save my Provence lavender seeds from the blossoms and my friend has an overloaded lemon tree." He's made me happy and smiles. Then waves goodbye to leave for his countrified city place, filled with the aromas of Samovar's teas, I'm sure.

I leave and cross the street to peruse the SFMOMA. I've been wanting to see the Richard Avedon photography show for months and it's about to close. I look at the fashion model with the elephants, the boy with bees on his skin, Richard's own father wasting away before the camera, a spiky one of his wife, and head shots of politicians, including presidents and senators and then there's one of Janis Joplin in full regalia smiling into the camera and so young you would never believe she would overdose on heroin and a few other selected drugs only a few years later. Her own version of a maiden's ecstasy.

I shop for gifts at the Museum store and find a very cute Wayne Thiebaud counting book for my friend's new grandson and other great visual treats. The rain is pouring down now, so I decide to sip some red wine in the museum cafe, medicinal only, and wait out the storm. I notice a tall handsome man in a long classic trench coat. He seems to be doing the same, as I've seen him upstairs in the Avedon exhibit too. For some reason he notices me looking at him, and waves to me and as I leave, he leaves too.

"You look like a European, not like an American—maybe are you from Germany or Switzerland?" he asks as we walk along.

"Thanks, I consider that a compliment," I say, "but I have to confess to being a native Californian." I know it's the combination of the boots worn with a short skirt, and the beret that's giving this pseudo-European impression.

We both step out into the rain. "Oh, California girl," he says, "I like California. I'm from the land of cigars." "Cuba?" "Yes, and I miss it terribly. I'm just waiting for the day when I can go back. That's my home, you know." He suddenly looks pained, but still when I look at his chiseled pale face, I never would have guessed he was Cuban in a million years. I hold up crossed fingers, well, as crossed as I can get them these days, finger joints being what they are, and say, "I hope it's soon."

I turn to go down the alley. "Hey, are you going to the parking garage too?" I ask. "No, in here," he says as he steps into the lobby of a fancy bank. "I'm doing business now," he says closing the bank door behind him as he waves goodbye. He too has taken a break for art and now it's back to the grind.

Somehow these exchanges with the different SF men have me smiling. They've brought out little red, they've brought out the snow whiteness of me. They've brought me my form of maiden's ecstasy. My husband and I share a veggie dinner at Greens on Fort Mason's dock, right near his software conference. "What did you do today," he asks. "Oh went to the art museum. I'll tell you about it later."

Six months later my husband and I are eating in the Union Hotel in Occidental and there's a very large group seated across from us.

"Jeez, what's the story?" I ask the waitress.

"They're here from a San Francisco restaurant," she tells us, but she doesn't remember which one. I can't resist, I lean over and ask a girl at the long table, "What restaurant are you from?"

"Samovar," the young woman says, "We came to do the ropes course at Ocean Song."

"Samovar, that's my favorite place to eat lunch in San Francisco!" I exclaim. Then impulsively I ask, "Is Eric here?"

"Yes," she says pointing to the other end of the table. By this time, whether I want it or not, I have the whole table's attention.

"Eric," I get up to go to where he's sitting and shake hands. "I met you months ago and you were so nice to me, you gave me some delicious lavender lemonade."

He laughs. "I think I remember—you were coughing a lot, right?"

"Right," I have to laugh too.

"Well," he says getting up from the table and pushing his chair back. "We've got to get going, we've got a long ride ahead of us. Nice to see you. Come back to Samovar!"

Yes, they have a rainy hour and a half ride back home to San Francisco. They're leaving the forest for the city.

"How do you know Eric?" my husband asks when I sit back down. I tell him about my day in the city, about Eric, and the Cuban man, and the guy from LA. I tell him about the specially-named tea. I think it's good to occasionally remind a husband that other men have told you their secrets, and that they might even think of you as deep forest, with dark earth thrown in. He looks at me and winks. I can tell that he finds it more amusing than anything else.

White Duck Lost

After signs seen on Mill Station Road, 2005.

White Duck Lost. White Duck lost, hasn't been seen for weeks. She's missing from Mill Station, from Graton.

Posted, our white duck is lost, gone, flown the duck coop. We haven't seen her in the duck yard, at the watering hole or with birds of a feather. She's lost, our white duck, lost.

Maybe we should offer a reward for our white duck lost. And then she'll be found. The bastards who took her will bring her back. Or someone will recognize her from her white duck photo, which was not posted because all white ducks look alike.

But our white duck, Anna Belle, she's different. She's no regular white duck. Yes, she has wandered before, but she always came back and anyway, we took care of that problem by fencing her in and clipping her wings.

Anna Belle has a way, a certain waddle which tells her mood, and a modulated quack, which sounds like an old Chinese laundress I once saw in a movie, calling to her daughter-in-law. Stressed and insistent, and sometimes downright shrill.

White Duck Lost, with our phone number posted, but the phone never rings and I'm wringing my hands wondering what happened to Anna Belle. It wasn't even mating season and she's been gone for six weeks now.

I can't stand the thought of the black crows, the gnarly buzzards, the dogs or other bone pickers finishing off a bite of Peking duck at the expense of our Anna Belle. Or the flattened feathers from her tail flying up with the passing of each car.

No, that's not what's happened to Anna Belle. There is no sign or scent or trace of that kind of thing. Maybe someone needed a good duck to take care of the mosquitoes; there is West Nile Virus, after all; or to pluck bugs off plants in the garden

Anna Belle is so very good at de-bugging, in addition to the way she loves to eat the left-over limp lettuce and crop back the weeds. I'm pulling them now and it isn't any fun for me. Anna Belle seemed to love it.

White Duck Lost, missing. Perhaps eaten by a wolverine, or a mountain lion, a bobcat or a raccoon, a coyote, or a hungry Mexican worker, far from his wife and children living in the arroyo and eating off of a sooty campfire grill. Maybe someone is wringing her neck.

White Duck Lost forever gone. No more paddling around the muddy pond, head ducking in and out, sifting the bottom for edibles. No more following me as I fill the dish with grain and greens collected from the local restaurants.

No more Anna Belle, the chefs will say as they toss scraps into the garbage. Too bad your White Duck is gone. We know Anna Belle was a good white duck.

Ah, too bad.

Not gone, I'll say, White Duck Lost says the sign and that says it all. Not gone, just missing. And soon I'll take down the signs. White Duck Lost.

Saint Francis and Bo the Dog

This small St. Francis, covered in a patina of moss and mold, holds a cement squirrel and a cement dove in his cement arms. He was sitting outside the local antique store, and even though I'm not a religious person, his look drew me in. His eyes searching upward, seeking, beseeching heaven. I felt pulled toward him. Maybe his angst-filled expression, his mood of distress, reminded me of my ill-fated first husband—always suffering.

St. Francis has a particular job—to protect animals and birds. His namesake is my favorite city, San Francisco. I placed him at the entry steps to our house where I could see him if I wanted to, out the glass of the front door.

Later the same day of the St. Francis purchase, towards evening a horrendous storm arrived. Trees thrashed around, rain pelted down and the storm's lightning was accompanied by amazingly loud thunder so close to the house, to the woods near us, that a few times I'd been down on the floor covering my ears. I was practically howling. A primal instinct. Thunder made the entire house shake. I shouted for Forrest to come home from his friend's—as though he could hear me—so he could hold my hand and tell me not to worry.

Since Bo hadn't reacted to thunderstorms in the past, I assumed that she was one of those rare dogs who was not afraid. I believed that she was nested comfortably in her rugs in the doghouse, under a large overhang on the patio. She lived outside due to a combination of my allergies and my husband's belief that's where dogs belonged. She had been living outside since the day she was born and she seemed comfortable there.

Maybe she'd been barking to come in, or sticking her broad face through the cat door in the garage, a relic from the previous owners—a sign that she wanted in—but I didn't hear her and I didn't know she was gone.

In the morning I called her to come for her treat, and then breakfast. Our ritual for years. The biscuit a reward for a job well done—protecting us through the night. I whistled and called some more. No luck. Of course it was still storming, winds bending the trees and rain pouring into the back gardens. I figured it might be hard for any dog to hear me, but that was just a way to avoid the obvious—Bo was gone; she was MIA.

An escape artist—Bo nudged the wire fence until she was able to squeeze underneath. Her goal was usually a visit to the little boy on the property across the fence who loved Bo. He liked to pet her and gave her treats. He was a sweet special needs kid, and gentle with Bo. I'd been meaning to fix the fence, but I never seemed to find an easy or inexpensive solution, so I kept putting it off. I phoned the next-door neighbors with the little boy. They said that Bo was not there; I had to widen my search.

The hunt for Bo begins in earnest when I pull on boots caked with mud and toss on my yellow slicker. I go everywhere we usually walk together in our rural neighborhood. "Bo, Bo," I call, barely audible in the funky winter weather. Then I start to hike the trails, and the orchards and the forest behind my house. I call my husband at work, and my three daughters, my stepson and daughter-in-law, and everyone I can think of. I phone, or knock on the doors of all my neighbors, "Have you seen my dog, Bo? She's smart—an Australian Shepherd, Border Collie mix, black with brown markings, almost like she's wearing a bow tie. She's been missing since the thunderstorm last night." But no one has seen her.

I slog all over the place. Rain creates a rivulet across my face where it falls from the hood of the slicker. I step over fallen branches, into thick redwood duff, trounce through big puddles and potholes filled with muddy water. My white hair frizzes out. I stop once, very hopefully, to look at a paw print, a large dog, maybe larger than Bo. Funny, I don't really know what her paw prints look like and I'm not sure I would recognize a mountain lion print either.

One neighbor, Lola, who is about 90 years old and from New Zealand, says she heard a dog barking in the storm and that her daughter, saw a dog and "a strange animal, probably a bobcat, definitely NOT a mountain lion" over in the apple orchard across the street. This causes my heart to speed up, beating in sync to the tune of, *Not a mountain lion, not a mountain lion.* But still there is no trace of Bo. Lola calls several times, "Have you found yer dog? I lost a dog once, one I really loved. And once a cat, torn to shreds in my yard."

"Thanks for your concern, Lola," I say as my head spins around. *Too much information,* I mutter to myself, something my kids often accuse me of. Lola says it wasn't a mountain lion, but this summer a neighbor saw one on the road and another running up the very lane where Lola has seen the two creatures. I look through the photo albums for a picture of Bo and put it on my alter with a little pile of dog biscuits.

My neighbor Mike is noisy and full of neighborly love for Bo. He and his wife Barbara give Bo a morning treat, they confessed last year, and they've been doing it for the seven years of her life. "Bo-Bo, Bo-Bo." I hear Mike call as he circles around, on his little golf cart cum tractor known as an Alligator for its green color. He drives down in the fields and valleys and woods. Even though I haven't asked, both Mike and my son-in-law say they've gone to the animal shelter, and she's not there. Later I bounce around in the alligator with Mike. Two of my three daughters and I all think that she's gone down where the orchard and a huge gully with a stream come together. Mike on a mission, pummeling downhill as fast as he can go until we get caught up in a thicket of wire fences and can't go further into the canyon. *Oh boy my back will hurt tonight,* I think. After dark a young neighbor calls to say she's hearing a strange barking down in that same valley just above the local school. We get in the car, and drive down her driveway and try to hear over the wind, but all we hear is a pack of coyotes. We do live in the woods. We share the terrain with raccoons, rabbits, deer, foxes, coyotes, bob cats and mountain lions. Oh yes, and rattlesnakes, like the one that killed another dog this summer, just down the street.

"Animals hate thunder," Mike says, "She's somewhere around here—she just freaked." Once this happened to him and he found his two dogs miles away from home. I don't know whether to hug him or hang my head and cry. And when I talk to my daughters I find myself saying things like, "I never did know how to watch out for babies or animals, or how to take care of things." "Mom, get a grip, the dog made a hole in the fence and ran off!" They don't like to think of me as benignly neglectful. But recently my two-year-old granddaughter, Sadira, almost ate a mushroom up by my studio. I don't know if it's a common field mushroom or a death cap. How are we to know every dangerous thing? I do know that Bo's tags are old, if they're still on, and probably unreadable. And there's the hole in the fence I knew about and could have repaired but didn't. Ah, remorse hits me hard.

Fortunately, the storm has not taken out the power as so often happens when we have a combination of high winds and rain. The trees that fall have not fallen on power lines. I'm still able to email and print up a flyer with Bo's picture. I happen to look up from my desk to see the calendar hanging above. I buy one every year because I love the art. It always features drawings of the year's Chinese Zodiac animal. This year, 2003, is the Year of the Dog. Last month's motto was: *Throw away what holds you back,* with a jubilant dog dancing away from his collar. This month's, I notice on this second day of March, is: *When lost, bark loud,* with a rather perplexed, or perhaps terrified dog in the woods. Ouch. Then I read the poem *Lost,* which is tacked next to the calendar on the wall above my desk. It ends: *Stand still; the forest knows where you are. You must let it find you.*

My littlest grandkids, ages one and two, and their dad and uncle take the 4-wheel and the uncle's dog Solomon to search for Bo. They explain that they try to think like dogs in wind and hail; try to get the other dog to catch a scent and bark and invite. The 4-wheel can go almost anywhere around here without getting stuck. Still, no sign of Bo, the other dog has not coaxed her out.

My good friend Terry says, "Go to the animal shelter and take a picture of Bo." So Forrest goes to Santa Rosa to deliver the picture. I post more flyers all over, pinning them to signs and power poles. It's still damp out, drizzling, so I have each flyer encased in plastic wrap. One pole has a sign for "White Duck Lost," but nearly every place I put a sign there's a sign that says, *Lost, Manx cat, Reward,* with a phone number. I've seen these same signs for months. I move these weather beaten signs to make room for mine. What is wrong with this person? Obviously her cat is GONE. I angrily pound tacks into my "Have you Seen Bo?" signs. Later when I post a sign at the local brick-oven bakery, I meet the Manx cat women. She's putting up another sign. "Don't you think you're cat is gone?" I ask, "Aren't you going to quit looking for him?"

"No" she says. "I will never give up on my cat." I wonder if I'll be so persistent and positive. It's Friday and now Bo's been gone a night and almost two full days.

I've had bad luck with my dogs. Two were shot by sheep ranchers, and a third one, a protective chow mix, had to be put down after biting a bunch of guests and then pulling my dad off the deck, breaking his hip and shoulder. Bo was different right from the start. She was eager to please and intelligent and the first dog I'd thoroughly trained since her puppyhood, when she slept for a few weeks in a box in the kitchen until we had a safe place for her outside. She let me, along with Forrest and son, Lee, be her alpha guide to life. And she only dug up plants and chewed through one flashlight handle in her adolescent phase. She is about the most perfect dog ever. Oh Bo!

Next day, it's not only raining, there is intermittent hail as I hike the forest behind my house down to the giant pond, nesting spot of large gray herons. A vineyard now owns the land and they have put in a lot of new roads and seem to be building a bottling plant across from a hundred-year-old Victorian farmhouse. I imagine Bo snagged by the collar in a barbed wire fence of a sheep ranch, or shot dead by a rancher who needs no real excuse except he raises livestock for a living. Maybe she had a fight with a raccoon and is in hiding, licking her wounds. She's smart and a survivor; I've seen her catch and eat squirrels, birds and rabbits. She'll be okay, I tell myself. But when my husband checks with the Humane Society to see if there's any news, and there's not, I burst into tears. The wind has died down but it's still raining and cold, and Bo's out in it somewhere. I just can't bear to think about it.

I slug down a shot of brandy and have a restless night's sleep. I dream of Bo walking at my side, ears blowing back, nose into the wind for the scent of something interesting. I'm so disappointed to wake up. No Bo.

Saturday morning, like a child might, I move St. Francis into the bushes where I can't see him. "You didn't do your job," I practically scream at him. I drive down to the school below and call and whistle for a half hour without any signs of her, even though I think I hear a faint barking above me.

About 3:30 in the afternoon on Saturday I go to my altar, "Bo, make your presence known to me, let me know where you are, please, please." I beseech. The phone jars me. It's a volunteer from the County Animal Control center in Santa Rosa, "A man just brought a dog in, and I think it's yours. It looks just like the picture." I can hear a man in the background saying, "Fiori Lane, why that's up above me."

"Let me talk with him," I say.

He asks, "Is your dog's collar purple?"

"Yes, yes!" I say, my hopes up high.

"And she's furry and dark and a real sweetheart?"

"That's Bo!" I yelp.

"Well, they're just about to close here, you want me to just bring her back with me?"

"Oh would you? I can meet you at Salmon Creek School."

"Okay, how about at 5:00." He tells me that Bo has been found down below the very canyon we all have dreamt about.

"Thank you so much," I say, my voice crackling— the words barely cough out.

I'm at home by myself, and damp from hanging posters out in the rain. I'm jumping up and down and don't know whom to call first. We have no cell phones, and no cell connection, so there's no way to call my husband who is waiting for our son who's attending a self-help meeting in Santa Rosa. I call my daughters one at a time and then my other son and daughter-in-law. They are all elated. They love Bo too, even though she doesn't drop the ball when she's asked to, and sometimes she sticks her nose in their crotches and they yell at her and smack her on the nose. I also phone my neighbors, starting with Mike and Barbara.

"That's fantastic news," Mike says. "We love Bo-Bo."

And then I move St. Francis back up to the front porch place of honor and pick a flower to put at his sandaled feet.

When we meet, I spontaneously hug Bo's savior and give him an art print, a thank you card, and some wine. "I never knew I could love a dog so much," I confess.

"Get the dog some new tags," he scolds.

"I will, I promise, and thank you again."

"I've had dogs," he says. "I know how you feel."

Bo seems antsy and freaked and whines all the way home. When she gets home, she drinks a lot of water and then scratches her back on the wet lawn before she limps into her doghouse to sleep. "I'm so glad you're home," I say to her softly. She doesn't even stir or vaguely wag her tail.

I'm making family dinner in celebration. Every 10 minutes

I go out to check on Bo. "How are you girl? We're so glad you're safe." Still, she's sound asleep—snoring a little and her legs shaking occasionally. She had a really long walk and I'll bet she was afraid too.

We have shoved a garden rock into the hole in the fence and put a lawn chair in front of that for good measure, but I promise myself that this fence will be my project as soon as the weather improves.

My granddaughter greets everyone at our family dinner, with, "We found Bo and she wasn't eaten by a mountain goat." When everyone howls with laughter she seems upset.

"I know," I say, "I'm glad too. No bobcats, or mountain goats or even mountain lions got our Bo." Little Saben gets the closest he's ever been to the dog, and Bo licks him—his first dog kiss. He looks at me with wide eyes, seeming to cry, but then bursts into a big smile, "Bo the dog," he says in his gravelly one-year-old voice.

The next morning Bo is in a deep sleep, barely interested in getting her morning treats. I look out the front door, more rain. There stands St. Francis, looking anguished. Now I get that look. It's about responsibility for all small creatures on the planet. It's about being so small yourself with such an enormous job to do. I understand.

Wild Flour

I'm not the only one—there's a line out the door today at Wild Flour Bread. The place smells of wood smoke, burnt sugar and garlic. While the bread's not the best I've ever had in my life, it's good hearty West County sour dough bread, baked in a French style brick oven and served by friendly, dancing bakery employees.

There's happy music and the staff is busy either kneading dough, brewing coffee and chai drinks, or handing out bread samples to a stream of eager people. The employees, a mix of old and young, men and women, are funny and friendly, irreverent and hip.

The Wild Flour has been in Freestone as long as I've lived up on the hill above it, 14 years now. I've seen them slowly form a steady loyal clientèle and suddenly explode into a phenomenon: people in line from Texas, from Washington DC, from Paris, from San Francisco. They're all here for the

aromatic breads, but fed too, by the ambiance. In a world growing more monochromatic every day, this unique place offers
color and spices. A big elephant is painted next to the oven,
and birds—swallows flying out and around the oven's chim-
ney, sea gulls settled on the beams, and wide-eyed owls—
painted on the walls and ceiling in an inspired moment by an
employee in the middle of the night.

I remember when the building used to be a grain and feed
store with a gas pump and burger joint attached—Rocco's—
with Maria standing over the grill, her cleavage one of the main
attractions. Wild Flour sits in the fertile bowl of the Freestone
Valley, a small rolling-hilled Shangri La, which in the winter
could be a cousin to green Western Ireland. Across the street
are cattle and an iconic barn with red silo immortalized by a
million painters. Last time I was here, friends of mine were
across the street plein aire painting, standing in the field with
black and white cows who soon clamber after a feed truck.

The gas pump is gone and in its place are racks of hats, scarves
and a few choice antiques at the aptly named "Enduring
Comforts." Inside are crystal and brass candle sticks, rows and
bins of candles, pottery from the 1920s, modern Italian linens
and sterling silver jewelry. World music beat or classic jazz
plays, and if you like what you're hearing you can purchase
the CD.

Beyond the parking area is the Wild Flour garden in late
summer abundance. Today it's overloaded with huge sunflowers planted by my friend Sally, with an arbor of grapes, morning
glories and gourds. There are full beds of gigantic purple-red cab-
bages, curly leafed red and green kale, and beans on bean poles.
A spirit of generosity pervades. Kids, especially, are invited to
pick as many as they want of the raspberries and strawberries.
When my granddaughter comes with me, she always says, "Let's
see what's in the garden that we can eat or smell."

Inside, guests are courteous to each other and chat, comparing their bread choices. Bicycle clubs stop for a snack, and

to use the bathroom, with its colorful stained glass window. "I love that painting in the bathroom, Gramma, you should go in to see it," says my young grandson. He knows as an artist I'll appreciate the window's beauty. I try to explain the concept of a stained glass window but give up and just say, "I know, it's glass, and I agree with you, it's beautiful. I love it too."

This bakery is a kind of a welcome mat, or more a front door to the quirky, welcoming, foody environs of the West County. The owner, Jed, plays drums in a salsa band, surfs, and loves to travel. Once a year he closes down the bakery and the whole Wild Flour goes camping. The nine, or sometimes more, employees all take time off to vacation with the same people they work with. Just another different concept fostered by Jed Wallach. He only opens for the long week-end, saving at least three days a week for surfing, salsa music, or other pursuits.

The help get paid a decent wage and are part of something that's becoming a modern legend. A place that doesn't advertise except with a couple of sandwich boards out on Bodega Highway. Word of mouth brings people in, and some of those people are travel journalists and TV folks and soon Jed has all the business he can handle. There's a tip jar overflowing and a sign that says, "We knead ones." Meaning everyone has come with twenty dollar bills to pay for their $3.50 scones or their $5.00 and $6.00 breads. Even CNN has run a feature on Wild Flour.

There's a long table so that people can sit while they wait, or like me, eat something yummy together with other people, strangers usually. I make it my practice to try to really connect with someone—a stranger—at the table. Learn about their lives, where they're from, what brings them to Wild Flour. Okay, so maybe I have "boundary issues," but I hold it as part of an odd spiritual practice of reaching out. As a retired counselor, I miss hearing people's stories, getting to know someone else's life.

On the table is a metal scale with two bowls and a basket of rocks. Kids and adults get a kick out of trying to balance the scales by adding rocks on either side. There's a plastic cash register to entertain small kids. The register was used for real until recently, when the heavy volume of sales required a modern electric cash register. And it's cash only here, checks or real money please, no plastic. But if you don't have real money with you, you can simply send in the money later—it's an old-fashioned honor system. "Bring home a sticky bun," my husband requests when he finds out where I'm headed on a Saturday morning. Loaded with cinnamon, raisins, sugar, butter and nuts, a sticky sugary glaze gives the ample bun its name. More like a loaf, it's square and decadently delicious so that you feel kind of like you're a kid again at Gramma's when you eat it. I've watched people cut it up into pieces and sit down at the long family-style table and eat the whole thing, bite by delicious bite. "Sure, okay darling, good for the diet!" I answer. I know the loaf can miraculously last almost the week with its solid sour dough base. Unless we eat it all when I return.

Sweet breads and scones are the first to come out of the oven in the morning, followed by crusty savories a few hours later. Cheese breads, the goat herb and fougasse, and everything in between, all made from a mother batch of sourdough that is kept alive in the bakery. There's no shortage of garlic and herbs here, no shortage of seeds to line the tops of the loaves, no shortage of flour, which covers the long kneading table. Everything is right before our eyes, all phases of the making of the bread is there, transparent for all to see. European style, the breads are stacked up and fanned out on a table in front of the tasting bins, while the ones just out of the oven are lifted on long wooden paddles and left to cool in racks, sticky sugar, or gooey cheese dripping off the papers.

Usually it's the scones I'm after. Often there's just a little chocolate thrown in with the fruity bread dough. And things from the garden in season, and from the area, plums, apples, and even ginger to spice up a cool foggy morning. To go with the scone, I want a chai latte, hot in winter and iced in summer. On days when I can, I take them with me ten minutes down the road to the beach, the Pacific Ocean calling me for a walk where I sip the chai and watch surfers, gulls, sandpipers, dogs, and sometimes horse back riders.

The Wild Flour addresses a basic need for tribe, for wholesome organic ingredients, for being in on a certain now well-known secret with all the others there. People are in a good mood, they're getting free samples and bread buying is simply contagious. I volunteer, "The hazelnut and white chocolate apricot scones are scrumptious!"

"Can I have a sample?" A woman asks.

"So sorry," the employee with the Australian accent says, "but I can give you some yummy Bohemian bread if you want it, love."

"Take a chance on a scone," I say, showing her what mine looks like.

"I will," the woman says," Her husband says, "Make mine sticky bun."

My three bigger grandkids want the hot chocolate at holiday time. And they want the little bread stars or turkeys made on the whim of the bakers. Someday the twins will join in the sweet fun too.

Things here are simple and easy, free, and then decently priced, fun and family like. It's sort of a throw-back to the olden days—nothing mass-produced about it. There's a gigantic mound of dough rising in the middle of the table and being shaped into submission, pummeled into seeded French, or rye or a simple country loaf, rectangular and suited for toast or sandwiches.

One day the garden maker, and bakery morning manager, friend Sally is off for the day. Her son, Ben, has been badly burned fighting a fire in nearby Bodega. A downed live electrical line sending a jolt through his body, burning his hands and numbing the place where the current exited his body.

Everyone is concerned and there is a benefit planned for a few weeks from now. Next time I'm in, Sally's working and she's positive. "He's getting good treatment in San Francisco. He's going to be all right."

"He's one of our heroes," I tell her. Out here almost all our firefighters are volunteers and we depend on them, and appreciate their sacrifices, their dedication. She'll bring bakery bread to the benefit breakfast and everyone from all over the place, who passes through this small dot on the planet will know of the benefit through Wild Flour, and hopefully, the dollars will trickle in from all over the world. It's that kind of place.

When any of our five adult children visit, the Wild Flour is on their list of to-do's. Same for the grandkids. And always, for us. One time Jed, the owner, sees Forrest and I sharing a scone and winking over a fun moment. Later when I come again he says, "It was so nice to see the love between you and your husband. I've kind of given up on love lasting, marriage

and all that." I'm taken by surprise. I explain we've both been married before, a couple of times even, and we've had plenty of professional help, counseling, to help us through the stormy times. We're committed to stick it out, see it through. It's sugar, and white chocolate tucked into layers of yeasty dough I think. "We're not a perfect fit, and it's not always roses, roses," I say to Jed, "but we know what we want, what we've got, and we're still interested in each other, still in love." He smiles at me the whole time I'm talking. A kind of skeptical smile, but a radiant smile. He, after all, is the mother dough of Wild Flour. He's what pulls it all together. It's his vision, his love that has made this place, my home away from home in the drizzle of winter and go-to spot in the summer. He is the sweet and savory of the bakery. And he's made a place where everyone feels the love.

A Bee Line

What I see today disturbs me. I'm used to watching a bird circus out the back window—a real *Field Guide to Western Birds* display out there. Birds dive down from the trees—redwoods, birch, madrone, Texas privets—to drink from my fountain, or take a little bath. Sometimes competition breaks out between the large, clumsy pigeons, and the smaller birds. The most common visitors in summer are tiny bright yellow and black male goldfinches. Like small dogs, hummingbirds, nuthatches, and finches are fiercely territorial and aggressive. Even the fat robins will give over their lip of the fountain to the little guys.

The pigeons and towhees tend to land right on the finial where water burbles out. The hummingbirds are more cautious and snatch water as they fly by. But, today the fountain offers a different scene. For one thing, it's messy. The sides look like they're completely caked in a muddy mold. What the heck is happening?

I go outside to investigate up close and personal, and what I find are hundreds of little golden honey bees perched in messy clumps all over the smooth concrete rims of the two-tiered medium-sized fountain. They're filling up on water. The day is nearly 100 degrees and the bees will perish without water. I know that they must cool their hives. I'm concerned about bees and have been reading a lot about "colony collapse" in the newspaper. Between Monsanto's messing with the genes of plants, creating ever more powerful pesticides, and the naturally occurring pests to bees, like mites, bee hives are crashing. I feel happy that somehow I'm part of the bees' good cycle today.

Goldfinches hop among thin drooping birch tree branches. They're fussing—lots of chirping going on. They've decided to give over and wait. They've determined that the bees are more needy than they are. Or maybe they don't want to get stung. A bee can kill a bird with its sting.

Bees sip and sip, and then fly off, directly over the roof of the house back to their homes—stacks of white hives in my neighbor Chad's apple orchard. Now I've seen a bee line—a determined flight, efficient, and mathematical—that straight-line-shortest-distance-between-two-points math. It's not the whirling, exuberant pollen dances of the bees in nature films. This is serious business and their mission is dramatic with no time for wasted movements or wrong turns. Waiting at home are their babies tucked into geometric beds in danger of dying from the heat. Bees need water to fuel the beating of hundreds of little bee fans—their own wings—humming away to cool down the beehive. A wingathon is happening, like the most effective swamp cooler imaginable.

I know about this fanning technique because my husband tells me. Forrest's uncle kept bees at his Missouri farm in the Ozarks and explained it all to him when he was a was kid.

As soon as one group streaks off, a new wave of bees arrive. It's the first time since we put in this fountain three years ago, that we've been inundated with thirsty bees. Between the heat and the bees' thirst, the level of water goes down rapidly. They are so focused that even when I walk right next to them with the green garden hose, they pay no attention to me. I gently add some water to the fountain. I don't want to disturb them. Secretly, I'm a little afraid they may decide to go after me.

Bees clump all over the fountain looking like an untidy spill. They leave no space at all for birds now. Not a round fat quail with its topknot bobbing around—not even a light fluttery orange butterfly, disturbs the bees. It's like they have an unspoken agreement about who gets the water.

I had no idea I'd host bees today, or at least, such an crowd of thirsty bees, but I live in Eve's neighborhood, an abundance of apples everywhere around me. The apples need the bees, who buzz through the neighborhood in spring crawling in and out of pink, white, and striped reddish blossoms. They take their time. They exit with legs loaded down by a cumbersome fuzzy golden ball of pollen, and they fly off in a sort of staggering pattern to the hive. As they go from flower to flower they pollinate. We all understand—that's what they're made for. We humans just happen to steal the nectar they create in their hives as a bonus. Honey, golden and sticky sweet. I'm sure that when bears roamed more freely here, they lucked upon a honey comb now and then, but the honey was probably a strong, dark honey, a sage honey, or perhaps nectar that tasted lightly of blackberries but not the even lighter amber apple blossom honey.

At our Occidental Farmers Market there's often an apiary guy selling local honey, the wildflower honey particularly strong and not so good in tea. Also, bees wax candles and soaps and even lip balm and bee products for babies too. He's a beekeeper, part of the brave, proud group who host bees year-round. They don their white suits, and sometimes the ladies put on more glamorous netted hats, and then they smoke the hives. Sleepy bees come out to see what's up and then their honey is taken. Just enough is left to maintain their babies.

In all my gardening, I've never been stung by a honey bee. I've collided with a few, and still, they've left me alone. I've always thought they knew I was the one putting in the lavender, roses, honeysuckle and the red pineapple sage they love. I have had stings from ground bees and other yellow jacketed types and they were nasty, sometimes getting infected from the carnivorous habits of these critters. I dislike them immensely and see them on a par with cowbirds who are too lazy to raise their own young. In summer when we eat outside, the yellow jackets hover, sometimes boldly landing right on a plate of food. I usually pick off a piece of something they like, like salmon, and put it out to the side to distract them away from the plates. Sometimes I even buy traps for these insects and hang them above the picnic table.

I know that venom from the bee family can cause allergic reactions. I was in Oregon at a B and B when the owner said she had to leave for Portland to be with her 21-year-old son who had just lost his best friend to a bee sting. It's scary stuff. My sister got sepsis from a bee sting, her hand swelling up like a fat clown's glove, and then a red streak inching its way up her arm. And a close friend lost her husband to a sting. Still, I feel pretty relaxed around bees, even when they are thick in my flowering lavender plants.

I was only scared by bees once, when my grandson Sky and I got caught in a swarm—bees everywhere around us, and so noisy and so many. Bees leaving home for a new spot. Thousands of bees sent packing. We ran for shelter, but the swarm just continued its bumbley flight across the pastures and into the forest. They pretty much ignored us. Around here in the west county, some beekeepers would try to follow the bees and come to snag the swarm for their hives. Free bees. No need to send away for a queen bee from Italy.

A part of me is pleased that I can help save bee babies, and a part of me misses the beauty of the little finches. The bees are so intense and determined, while the finches seem playful and colorful, sparkles of water-drops flicking off their wings. A simple birdbath versus life and death. And today, sweating in the heat, I'd rather not be thinking about the possible death of bees and their babies. I'd rather sit under the trees reading a book, sipping my honey-laced tea and looking up once in a while to see the beauty of the garden. After all, I'm retired now.

The bees are responsible for a good crop, as much as the rain and heat. We wouldn't have much to eat without them, no fruits, no almonds, all the things I really love to eat. Even clover for the dairy cows. But tomorrow, I look forward to a cooler day without bees—without their big neediness. I want the pretty finches back, or I'll even settle for the random wobbly funny quail or a messy Fiori Lane pigeon.

I'm scattered right now, and done in with caring for people and things and I don't even want to see a bee line. I'm taking a break from productivity, taking a rest after years of counseling others, raising a family and taking care of beloved grandkids. I just want time for myself this week. I prefer to see the bees in their wild frenzied directional dances, sharing the map to the best nectar, the new home. I can't think about bee death, about babies in jeopardy. Forget being a bee heroine, give me the sunny finches, the zooming hummingbirds, even the noisy brilliant blue jays. That's what really brightens my day.

High Flying Times in the Tall Trees

The 1970s and 80s were rampant with high times—an abundance of drugs of every color, shape, size, and substance. And each one offering a different effect, a particular high.

The Vietnam War disillusioned a whole generation of us, and weather-beaten "Question Authority!" bumper stickers were a common sight in western Sonoma County. A lot of professional people, responsible adults—as well as a bunch of irresponsible adults and even children—were all partaking of the high times. Some of the sheriffs were even lighting up joints. We lived in the hills and were hidden from view. We thought we had permission at the West Pole.

Adventurous folks sucked white powder through short straws off of little mirrors, or sniffed through rolled up hundred dollar bills. In one particular instance, friends of mine snorted lines of white powder off of the newly implanted silicone breasts of a friend. She was laughing and getting a kick out of it. I have to admit to being fascinated and shocked by her attitude, all at the same time.

If you worried about ruining your nose and making a big hole in your septum, you rubbed the cocaine on your gums. I tried it twice and experienced a bright flash, a buzz that lasted for what seemed a minute. Not worth all the fuss and hard heart pounding. I was "high on life." I didn't want to foster bad drug habits or bad trips, I told myself. I was a mom, after all. Of course I didn't really consider pot a particularly "bad" drug.

Glass pipes and water burbling hookahs were taken out of their special hiding places in the backs of closets. Bags filled with withered peyote buttons, crusty looking—resembling eucalyptus pods on a bad day—promised amazing visions, if you could just get past the vomit stage. And LSD available and cheap, was embedded into little bits of papers. When we took the kids, or at least the teenagers, to a Grateful Dead concert, we were offered "hits" and "doses" that touted a trip where you would see everyday scenery in the psychedelic colors of the beautiful posters that advertised rock bands. Some of those posters made by local artist Stanley Mouse.

I have a friend who was treated with LSD as part of her psychotherapy, back when LSD was legal. She claims it really helped her open up to her subconscious and deal with childhood trauma. I recently read *The Harvard Psychedelic Club*, and the official biography of Steve Jobs. Many successful business people, and lots of folks in the arts are still open to expanding their consciousness.

Back then, I knew any trips I took would probably pull me away from my thin grasp on reality, but now, during an open-studio event, after seeing my studio and all the colorful paintings within, people quietly comment, "Wow, you must have done some great acid trips in your time." I hate to disappoint them but long ago I realized what my particular brain chemistry could create on its own. I learned I didn't need the extra boost.

Not to mention that being caught with marijuana, or "paraphernalia" could land you in jail and merit a felony offense on your record. Everyone knew the attorneys to hire, but it was expensive and time consuming, and could cost you a job. Still, many residents took the risk.

There are lots of stories from the era when folks were growing "weed" out in their woods. Pictures of huge hemp plants being confiscated at the Wheeler Ranch made the front page of the San Francisco Chronicle. Stories circulated and became myths.

In one story a guy who lived in a railway caboose wired his pot garden with motion detector lights. One night when the lights went on, he let out his barking dog who cornered two young kids, one the babysitter for the other, an eight-year-old. The twelve-year-old, worried about his babysitting charge, ran back home and called the sheriff. The sheriff arrived, with back-up crews, freed the younger kid, drove him home, and came back for all the pot plants. Best intentions went astray all the time. Or sometimes deer ate the crop.

There were funny moments, and dramatic moments, like the time I picked up a known dealer. Her car was being fixed and I was going in the direction of the car repair shop.

"Stop," she shouted as we started out of town.

"What, what is it?"

"I left my purse on the table at home!"

"I can loan you money for the car," I offered.

"Can you loan me $150,000.00 in cash?"

We turned around and got her purse, and then as we drove into town I worried about all that cash in the car with us.

Another time a fairly conservative friend, a Catholic, a Republican, a mom, decided to take a mushroom, which led to two, three then five, as nothing seemed to be happening. All of a sudden it hit her. She went running upstairs and climbed into her bed. We heard her shouting from on high, "When will it stop? Can I poop it out and have it be over with. Help!!!" Like an old person with dementia, help help help. We gathered around her and held her hands and said, "You're going to be okay." She was having an anxiety-ridden "bad trip."

Sometimes the Sheriff's Department or the local volunteer fire department has to transport someone to the hospital from a bad trip. Me, for instance, when I first moved here, after eating marijuana brownies at a party in 1977. "Tachycardia. Your body needs to re-set it's patterns—that's why you feel like you're going to pass out," the ER doc said, "Just jump up from the gurney and let it happen."

"No way, you're supposed to help me, help my heart stop racing!" I whined, clutching the gurney railings so tightly that my knuckles turned white.

"Okay, just relax, it will take time. We'll give you a Valium and hope for the best," he said, turning away. A too familiar scene for him, I thought. It seemed like he was feeling something between disgust and amusement. That's the way I first met my doctor at the local health clinic. I was referred from Palm Drive ER for a heart follow-up.

One acquaintance got busted bringing cocaine into the US from South America and landed in jail. This friend later became a successful wine broker, a favorite job—besides politics or real estate—for people who were formerly employed in the underground economy growing or selling drugs. The feds or the state regularly swept through the area. They mowed down peoples' pot fields, or took the pot, probably for resale in the case of one notorious local sheriff. In the month of September as the plants were getting ready to be harvested, helicopters started their fly-overs, "CAMP," we would mutter to each other. "CAMP!" (Campaign Against Marijuana Planting).

Friends got busted by well-intentioned neighbors who saw white unmarked U-Haul trucks drive into their neighborhood and called the sheriff. They got busted by someone taking a walk through the woods and coming upon a big patch. Sometimes the neighbor whose property had been high-jacked didn't squawk, as long as the grower gave him a cut of the profits. Mostly though it was the CAMP helicopter fly-overs that spotted the crops, even when tucked into a tall growing vegetable garden, or pruned down to match the height of the tomatoes. The technology invented for war, specifically Vietnam, was applied to the citizenry. It became a weapon in "The War on Drugs." Apparently only the government was allowed in the illicit drug business.

Wine, of course, is the current drug of choice, and lattes, but the pot culture still thrives at the West Pole. Sometimes there are shoot outs, and even today, areas in the woods of places like Cazadero are off limits for walking unless you want a bullet whizzing past you. People now mainly grow indoors instead of out in the woods and get medical marijuana licenses. Marijuana helps with pain, with nausea and it's used a lot by patients who have cancer. But far too often the indoor grow lights wiring causes building fires.

With the harder drugs, when someone has not paid off a cocaine cartel, or a methamphetamine cooker, they risk strangers showing up in their homes with guns drawn. If they're families, like the ones I worked with at the local community college, they've often lost everything to stay loaded—even lived on the streets with their young children. It's still the wild west, it's Chicago and Al Capone, its hippies gone to the dark side—or, as Bob Dylan said, out to make it rich.

There are as many intensely sad stories of addiction and lost souls as there are stories of people with cancer being helped, or people whose appetites improved, people having great sex or spiritual revelations. There is the down side of the drug scene, even the marijuana trade. Recently three men were killed in a pot deal gone bad and several families we know have had home invasions. And kids lose their motivation; they don't go on to do what they could have with their talents. They are mellowed out to the max.

Twenty years after the main high flying times, friends have Hepatitis C. You can get it from shared equipment, even sharing a tainted joint from an infected person, or a tainted straw. Maybe you had a cut in your nose, or a sore on your gums. Opportunity strikes a blow. Fatigue and liver problems and not very effective treatments follow the diagnosis. Or you

could say you got it from immunizations in Vietnam, or from acupuncture needles, or from a bad tattoo parlor, but usually it was from shooting up a drug of choice, or from straws and dollar bills and shared joints.

I know I'm not much interested in taking a toke on a joint any more. The drug culture never offered that much to me, but friends still smoke the occasional marijuana cigarette. I hope my grandchildren don't get started on the drug path; I have seen so many kids wrecked by drugs—even end up dead because of their drug ways. But at the West Pole, people still light up in public. Maybe we're more tolerant here or maybe we still feel we're not really beholden to the letter of the law.

Anyway, like I said before, I'm high on life. A walk in the woods—tall trees surrounding the path—or a walk near the Pacific Ocean with the fog climbing over the rocks brightens my day. Being out in the studio with paint all over my hands, watching the grandkids kick a soccer goal, walking on a trail—these are what make me feel happy. Oh, sex and a glass of wine still work too.

Songbird

I've come to Pt. Reyes National Seashore looking for answers. I relish the smell of salt and love hiking along reed-laden trails, cow parsnips growing as tall as my head. It's spring at the coast; just about the best time anywhere that you can imagine. Fecundity spills over into everything. I'm here attending a workshop, but I'm not sure I'm really getting what I need. What I'm looking for is a Tarot card from nature to show me what I need to do next.

At the end of the trail I lie down, wishing I could be naked, skin hugging into the sun's warmth. The sea roils in the background, and even though my head is comfortably nestled into a mound of sand, I think of the stinging nettles I saw as I hiked in. Soft and prickly at the same time. A lovely trick of nature. You want to touch them, but you know it will sting for quite a while afterwards.

I close my eyes and listen for songbirds. Their melodious, comforting and sweet arias. Songbirds, Claire the naturalist said on our morning walk, are disappearing in alarming numbers. Predators get them, or there's not enough food to go around. They lose habitat or else it's toxins. They sing to call to each other, for the sheer joy of the sounds and to warn others away from their territory. No wonder they're disappearing, I think, they need to toughen up. The songs need to be a little more raven-like, with no mistaking the message.

Wrens, on the other hand, are thriving. Bird people call them "L.B.J.'s," Little Brown Jobs, and Claire said they don't bother to differentiate them in a bird count. Too many and too much alike, they just wear out the bird watchers. I laugh imagining the watchers flinging down binoculars in disgust, "It's just another damn wren!" They're hoping for something exotic, something mistakenly migrated from Latin America or New Zealand. The familiar doesn't excite them like it did at the beginning.

Years ago I read a piece by a famous writer, "Beware the Little Brown Wren." I didn't get it then, being young and so sure of my beliefs about love, but now I do. You don't see it coming; seduction in a plain brown wrapper. A woman's intent can work wonders, and maybe she knows that she looks great with her clothes off. Brown everywhere, with dark areolas. I roll over onto my stomach and curl an arm under my cheek. It's not always the beautiful woman who's after your man.

When you see a pack of small birds right on the tail of a big one, they're trying to peck out it's feathers, so it can't fly and come back for more eggs, or put eggs in their nests like the cowbirds do. Trickster of the bird world, cowbirds are big, and they sneak their big eggs into the nests of unsuspecting little warblers. The warblers struggle to keep up with the monster babies' demands, neglecting the tiny mouths of their own babies, who die of starvation. The cowbird is the clear winner. It's lazy, clever, and sneaky.

Yesterday, I saw red-tailed hawks spiraling down. A beautiful, coordinated flight starting way up and going nearly to the ground. When I asked the naturalist about this, she said it's "trust building before mating." The male is showing the female that he is coordinated. He also shares food with her mid-air. He convinces her that he knows what he's doing and his talons won't kill her as he digs in during sex. Sometimes something so lovely can disguise an urgent and driving force that just won't be denied. If trust is destroyed, then does the female let him mate again? I decide that she wouldn't have to make this decision because she is clearly dead.

I sit up and look toward the hills, filled with new growth after a huge fire a few years ago. We were told that it takes a fire to re-boot seeds and the destruction has to take place right down to the earth where seeds lie waiting for extreme heat to germinate. The only things spared in a natural fire are plants, trees and animals in the riparian zone, the watery spots. I have no water in my astrological chart, so I won't be spared from my personal fire. It will have to burn down to the very bottom, until all the old is gone and tiny new green shoots, the little spines of new trees and shrubs come up out of the ashes.

I get up and brush off sand. As I walk through the meadow I gather grass, twigs, leaves and a bit of string. Maybe I'll construct three nests, two to confuse the predators, so they'll leave the real one alone. I join the songbirds. My song sounds a little shrill, but on tune. I'm singing at the top of my voice. I sing out my warning, *this is mine, don't take it*. I want it to streak over the hills to my home, rustling the branches of the pine and redwoods. My husband might look up from the book he's reading for a moment and notice that there is a stirring outside. Just a little wind in the trees, he'll note. Nothing really to worry about.

I accept my kinship with songbirds. I imagine my song so strong and loud, it drives out any little undistinguished wrens or brown-headed cowbirds that might be thinking about my real nest. I continue to sing until my throat is raw and parched.

As I drive the Coast Highway I hang on to the image of two small yellow tanagers perched delicately on a branch outside my cabin window yesterday, and the large albino deer, moon reflecting off it's back last night and try not to think of the dangers inherent in love and mating.

Bohemian Farmers Market

Halloween marks the turn to rain and dark months of winter here at the West Pole. There's been the usual speculation over the weather—if it will hold for this last night of the farmers market season. Fortunately this day near the end of October, is mild, with dark approaching at 6:30.

Each Friday, June through October, from 4:00 until dusk we West Puddlians flock to the Bohemian Farmers Market. We wander by green and rainbow-colored chard, red and golden beets, cut flowers with bees still buzzing around and toward the end of the season, huge orange pumpkins, some looking a lot like Cinderella's coach. We stop for a taste of arugula, spicy on the tongue. The tangy greens make salads come alive and, "Yes, I'll take a bag." All the produce is organic, even locally-raised meat— organic. I usually bag up a colorful assortment of potatoes, so different from the bland, dull brown baking potatoes of my youth. I pick out red and yellow onions and toss them in my African hand-woven shopping basket.

There are hand-made chocolates too—you can even sample one of the truffles. There's local honey and honey products, and smoked salmon. There are tastes of bread and cheeses, both goat and cow. The mild fragrance of hand-made soaps catches me. The woman who used to sell her soaps, molded into shapes inspired from nature, now sells to Whole Foods and doesn't come to the market anymore. There's a new soap dealer.

There are fruit tarts and turn-overs and farm-fresh preserves and jellies. I stroll along, plucking out what appeals, and what will fill my fridge or pantry so it will be at the ready when I need to prepare a meal, or provide something to an airbnb guest in our little cottage. Sometimes, even though I have a lot of flowers in my own garden, I just have to bring home a bouquet of black-eyed susans, sunflowers or gladiolas. They're too cheap and too colorful to pass up.

In the early months of the market I also load up on peaches from Ed, the peach guy who is often joined in his booth by Nick Gravenities, well-known blues musician—the very same guy who played the blues for us at our wedding. Nick eats the sweet juicy peaches. "Tastes just like sweet honey," he says holding one out to try before he and Ed turn back to trading stories and joking. Ed is a Vietnam vet with "a gal in every port," he says, or in his case now, a gal in every peach orchard in the Sierra foothills, or maybe at several farmers markets. Somehow this unlikely couple of guys bonded over peaches, over the sixties and laughter. Nick's wife Marcia always knows where to find her husband. He sings me the beginning of a song, "Oh Mary Lou, she stole my diamond ring, she stole the keys to my Cadillac car..." He thinks it's pretty funny and so do I, but more than that, I'm touched that this talented man who has backed up the likes of Janis Joplin and Paul Butterfield, and who has written hit songs is standing here eating nectarines and golden peaches in Occidental at the Bohemian Farmers Market and singing to me.

There are samples of hummus from the Hummus Guy. He looks like he might be from Turkey, and has the very best garbanzo bean hummus in the world. I sample roasted red pepper hummus, and basil and sun-dried tomato hummus, but decide on the traditional simple flavors of original hummus with just the right amount of garlic. And I toss in a bag of his freshly made pita chips to go with it for the next time I host the book club, or the writers' group, or the Dueñas, or the grandkids and their parents.

My hubby Forrest and I have been reading *The Gastronomical Me* by MFK Fisher and everything around me in the farmers market resonates with her tales of Dijon, France, of Paris, of cooking and learning how to pick out just the right vegetables and just the right baguettes for a day's meal. This market is our version of a European moment. It's our nod to gastronomes like MFK Fisher who knew fresh and local is best. It's also our new meet and greet spot, replacing the post office and Harmony School, when it was still in town.

There are two kinds of paella by Gerard's Paella— vegetarian and seafood/chicken. Gerard lives up the street from us, and cooked paella at the wedding reception we threw in our backyard for Rowan when she married her West African sweetheart. The paella bubbles in huge pans, embedded with crusty and shell-bound crustaceans, shrimp antenna peeking out above the sea of chick peas, onion, shiny bright red and golden peppers with chicken thighs, drumsticks and breasts all turning a rich-yellow from threads of saffron. The best rice is the crusted stuff from the very bottom of the pan. The paella line winds around the block. Every local knows it's never ready until 6 pm.

Lata makes fantastic Indian curries, and spicy round samosas that only mildly sizzle on your tongue. There are specialty Mediterranean vegetarian dishes, brick-oven pizzas, cookies and home-made ice cream. Friends Maria and Joe's granddaughter, fourteen-year-old Mac, has her pie stand—always sold out by the end of the day, by the piece or by the entire pie. This time of year it's pumpkin, or blackberry from berries she's picked and frozen, but last week she had buttermilk pie, creamy with a crust looking ever so home-made. Our fifteen-year-old grandson Sky visits Mac's booth every summer. This year, before we left home he changed into a nicer shirt, or at least a clean one, and then, just before we got to the pie stand, he put on his glasses for her. They're both bookworms and he thinks she'll think that the glasses make him look like Harry Potter. They've known each other since they were babies; but now they're relating differently. I would call it flirtatious.

Usually the music at the market is mellow, intended as background for buying produce, and talking with neighbors. Sometimes there's energetic fiddle music, folk songs, or soft French vocals sung by the Hurdy Gurdy man as accompaniment to his hand-cranked tunes. But tonight is different, tonight the music will dominate, will pound through the market and over the hills of Occidental. Tonight the Taiko drummers play.

As I walk down the street with my shopping bags full, carrot tops sticking out of one African basket and a bouquet out of the other, I find myself inadvertently walking in time to the drumming. The drummers vibrate the street in front of Howard's Station Restaurant where one long block of white tents and produce carts line the street. Little kids, including my two local grandkids seven and eight, lie on the asphalt street, closed to all through traffic for now, and watch fascinated as Asian and non-Asians, male and female drummers beat out rhythms in dance-like fashion, wildly swinging their long sticks timed just right to pummel a three foot taiko on a stand. They even twirl the drums around on their stands and clack the drumsticks together. Then, in a choreographed move, the drummers turn to beat on another taiko, trading drums and rhythms. They wear cropped Japanese print pants and short "happi" Japanese jackets with cloth belts tied tightly around their waists. They have twisted scarfs wrapped around their heads, just like my husband wears to tai chi to keep perspiration from his eyes. They continue to thwack the big drums and lift up their long thick taiko sticks rumbling out a rhythm that has everyone in a spell. It's not the San Francisco Japanese Tea Garden were talking here, it's two-block long Occidental. When it's time to go, it's hard to get the kids to leave with me. They're mesmerized.

Locals have streamed out of the hills, from out of the woods and tourists are here to admire the magical qualities of Occidental with it's slowly disappearing small town simple life. They must like it that even in Brigadoon you can buy a paella dinner, hear a taiko beat, gather ye lettuces while ye may, and celebrate the abundance of life lived simply and well. I think MFK Fisher would approve.

Sea Treasure

A vase, a dark treasure
not filled with ash and bone
but with hopeful blessings
and salt water smell,
Year of the Metal Dragon.

Opaque with butterflies
Buddha dwells within
his picture and
a dot.org address,
Modern Contemplation.

Rice spills out
pearls, coins and
wisdom strewn about
free for the asking,
But does anyone ask?

Dark Treasure

A splintery scrap of wood with remnants of cobalt blue paint, a child's yellow plastic shovel, brittle sea kelp, bleached a pale rusty orange from the sun. Hundreds of small smooth stones, tumbled glass fragments, sand dollars and shells from the Pacific Ocean. Sometimes placed around my gardens, sometimes put into a piece of art, or one time, woven into a wreath—driftwood with starfish and dried twisting kelp. Found over years of beach combing. It's a habit; as I walk the beach, my eyes scan for sea treasure.

On this particular day in February 2012, following a full moon night, the tide at Doran Beach is unusually low. I skirt along the water line when I see what appears to be the upper leg and shell of a large reddish crab. As I get closer, the crab legs morphs into a piece of red cloth fluttering on the breeze. Is that a turquoise-colored butterfly I see? Right there, glistening in the sun on a rounded surface? I walk faster. It looks like a vase. This could be a real find! Perhaps something from the tsunami? I've read that the California coastline will be filled with detritus from Japan very soon. Wooden chests have already beached in San Diego. A dock surfaced in Oregon. The earthquake and tsunami and nuclear disaster bring us gifts from the sea, but not the ones Ann Morrow Lindberg described.

The vase is metal, a golden copper hue, covered with elaborate cloisonné butterflies, colors still bright and strong. Cotton cloth, 5 different squares of different colors—what looks to be prayer flags—are wrapped around and seal the top, which is bound together with big rubber bands and tied with twisted twine. I pick it up to inspect it more closely. It's a real treasure, a real find for me this time, not just the random whole sand dollar, or the full clam shell with no flaws, but a colorful Asian vase.

After my tsunami theory, the next thought I have is that this could be an urn filled with ashes and bones, cremation remains thrown into the ocean off Bodega Bay. The vase with butterflies looks very Japanese to me. I hesitate for a minute. Should I leave it in the sand, or take it and explore its innards? Yes, of course, take it, and be mindful of its contents. I pick it up and it's heavy.

The vase has been in the water long enough for the lip to become tarnished, and for a small starfish to take up housekeeping. Clinging to the vase, the little red starfish covers a blue flower and part of a butterfly. I'm excited and am not sure what to do next. I'm bursting with the discoverer's proud energy. What should I do next? I need to ask a stranger, or anyone who happens along.

Two tall men who look like they're in their late twenties are walking towards me. Shirtless and drinking something from a paper bag, probably beer but maybe whiskey, each holds onto a big muscular leashed dog; one looks like a pit bull the other a boxer. The men are muscular too, and tanned.

"Hi what ya got there," the blond with the pit bull asks.

They make me think of Orpheus and Cerberus, the mythological three-headed dog with the tail of the dragon who guards the entrance to the underworld.

I hold up the vase, with its starfish tenant, its prayer flags and rubber bands.

"Hey," they say together. "That's really cool."

"I know—I just pulled it out of the sand and I'm thinking of opening it up."

"Yeah," the guy with brown hair says, "There might be rubies and diamonds in it!"

"Do you have something to cut off the rubber bands and twine?" I ask him.

"He's got a knife," nodding toward the blond with the boxer. And out of a pocket comes a big switchblade. I imagine drug deals and body guards, but here on this beach in the sunshine, these guys seem nice enough. Just a little buzzed from beer.

The guy takes his knife and pops off the rubber bands and twine and hands back my find. I pull off the cloth cover— unveiling five prayer flags—and under it, a plastic top, black and salty smelling. I notice that the top appears to have had a pin backing. That's a surprise and modern. I pry it off and turn the vase upside down, tapping it gently, and then harder, against the sand. Rice, whole uncooked kernels not yet fluffed up by sea water pours out. As I continue to knock the vase against the water-hardened sand, the starfish tumbles off and is washed out by the next wave. Rice? I'm kind of puzzled, but the pit bull's owner suggests, "Maybe a Chinese fisherman lost his lunch for the day. It went overboard." The two guys laugh and make me laugh too, and they pass their paper bag beer back and forth, each taking a long swig.

"Well we're going down to the other end; we hope we can let the dogs off leash. They're sweet, but people are afraid of them. They're especially wary of the pit bull." I notice the blond commands his boxer by light kicks to the dog's side with his long bare foot instead of using vocal commands. (Good if you're in the dark, or need to be silent I think.)

"What about other dogs?" I ask.

"No, trouble," the pit bull owner says, "these boys are friendly and they love other dogs." I don't say anything more except "Goodbye and thanks!" They wave and walk off. They have left the gates to Hades unguarded, and in fact, have helped open the way in.

I keep pounding and nothing but rice comes out until I see a small blue paper poking out of the rice. As I pull it out I see it is covered with neat rows of gold letters that look like

Asian characters. Later, my daughter Mary Lea will say that to her it looks Burmese or Thai and not Chinese. The paper stinks of something like fish oil, but to me, the paper seems to be a prayer.

I glance at my watch and remember that I need to pick up my two grandchildren at school. They are seven and eight and going to spend the night. They might like to share this adventure.

As I walk back to the car I'm bubbling over, "Look what I just found!" I say proudly to two women who are walking from the parking lot towards the ocean. "That is amazing," one woman says. "Maybe *Antiques Roadshow* could help you identify it if it's old. Whatever it is, lucky you."

A man in the parking lot says, "That's so neat, I've always wanted to discover something cool like that in the water."

I show it to a surfer who is taking off his wet-suit. "Maybe a funeral urn? Glad I didn't share a wave with it. I would have gotten clobbered!"

I put the vase, which now smells pretty strong, into a paper trash sack in my car and pull onto Highway 1. In Bodega, I pull over to see if Yueni, the seamstress from Korea is in her dressmaker's shop with it's vibrant fabrics, finely finished kimono-shaped jackets, vests of silk and linen. I think she might be able to identify the gold prayer characters.

She sticks her hands into the rice, doesn't seem to be bothered by the intense fishy smell of it.

"You know in very poor countries people put vases on their altars. They fill them with rice and other food, for a time when they might need to eat and as a blessing to ask that they always have a good harvest and enough to eat. This writing looks Japanese. It could be from an altar in Japan that got wiped out in the tsunami."

"Oh no," I say, "I don't like to think about that." I thank her for her opinion and get back in my car. My Japanese neighbors lost many friends in the 2011 earthquake and tsunami.

Altars destroyed, people and people's lives destroyed. "Oh my." For a minute I feel really sad.

On the drive to school in Freestone, I call Mary Lea and ask if it's okay for the kids to join me in unearthing whatever is in the vase. "I'll make them wear latex gloves from my studio," I promise. "Sure," she says, "I think they'll love it!"

At Harmony School, Saben, Sadira and I walk to the car and I tell them about my find. "Want to help me discover what's in there?" I ask, as I open the back of the car and show them the vase. "It's possible that it could have some bones or ashes from a person who's dead," I add.

"It's beautiful—but it kinda stinks," says Sadira backing away slightly .

"I think it's a miracle—I can hardly wait to see what's in there," Saben Jr. says

"We will treat it gently and with dignity because we don't know its purpose yet," I explain.

They nod, grinning big grins.

When we get home they first have to wash their hands and have something to eat and then we head up the hill with our treasure sack. I get green gloves from the studio for all of us and then we sit on the ground under a big fir tree and begin our exploration.

We all agree that the contents smell bad, but after we shake out an endless amount of rice, something that looks like fish fins have to be pulled out. Then as Saben pounds the vase on the ground some more, a clump shakes free. "A necklace," Sadira says. "Amazing," her brother chimes in.

We look the jewelry over. A small triangular shard of pottery with a black outlined fish on white china rimmed in metal, dangles from a fancy piece of carved stone strung onto white round beads with jet black square beads. The fancy scrolled stone, brittle from sea water, suddenly snaps in my hands. "Darn it!" I say, trying not to swear in front of the kids. To me the piece of jewelry seems contemporary and inexpensive, kind of like something I bought in Paris that was from China. Saben and I take turns pounding out more stinky rice. Sadira refuses to touch anything now and just sits back and looks on. But when a round carved white ring with a white stone rolls out, she claps and laughs, and we all are excited. "What's next?" Saben asks. By now the smell is overpowering us, so we get the hose and squirt the rice out of the vase.

More papers come out. One is a picture of an ornate seated Buddha. When I turn it over there is what looks like a Chinese horoscope symbol with a website at the bottom: "Yogichen.org."

There are several square pale papers with a small insert of gold or silver foil in the center. Prayer papers. I know because sometimes I use them for embellishments in art pieces.

My family believes in messengers, fate, kismet. What are they going to think of this treasure—what does it mean to me and for me? Something good, I hope, but it seems to be about death. It could be seen as a blessing, a gift. Hopefully, not a curse. All superstition I remind myself. But, to someone somewhere, a symbolic gesture.

We hear something metallic banging around in the bottom. We look at one another.

Another few taps, and more water, and six tarnished coins tumble out. An I Ching coin, four American quarters, and a penny. I can barely make out the year, 2007 on one quarter. I'm puzzled now. Except for the I Ching piece this is as American as can be and recent, from the computer era.

I ask the kids, "What do you think this is all about?"

"I think a girl died and the family put her favorite meal and jewelry in the vase to please her spirit and they went out on a boat and dropped it in the ocean. They were kind of sad," Sadira says.

"I think it was a girl too, but I think they just left the vase on the beach for the waves to take away." Saben says. We move most of the contents to the foot of my Quan Yin statue, goddess of mercy and compassion. It's getting dark so we go down to the house.

We all clean up and change clothes and turn on the computer where I post my find on Facebook and within an hour we are getting lots of "commons" as Saben calls them. It's exciting to see people respond to our post and both grandkids want me to leave the computer on so we can keep checking it for comments, for "likes." We turn it off at bedtime when we have about 30 responses to our photos and post.

"Maybe somebody will solve the mystery of our treasure! I can't believe it, it's incredible," Saben says. He's definitely the most excited over my find, but we are all cranked up over it.

I drive the kids to school in the morning and later in the day on Facebook someone has gone to the Buddhist website, Yogichen.org and found an announcement with pictures. When I click on the link, there's my vase—and 14 others like it, some with big flowers instead of butterflies. All the vases, lined up in a box, bright red cloth with rubber bands and twine, are being hauled out in a boat to be thrown into the sea near Bodega Bay.

A bored-looking boat captain sits by the wheel, while a monk-like man smiles at the camera of a man credited as "Dejong." The caption announces, "Releasing the lives of people born in Fire Dragon years." Puzzle solved. My sea treasure is a dark one.

I go up to the studio and look at the treasure. The pin-backed top that was black the day before has changed and now reveals a blue dragon with red flaming mane and goatee, ridden by a fierce-looking Asian warrior with shield and spear. The truth is out, the fire dragon appears and what's crazy is that this is the year of the water dragon in Chinese astrology.

When I ask my Facebook friends what I should do with my dark treasure, they say things like, "It was meant for you." "Put it your garden. "Bless it and return to the sea." And the suggestion I like the best, "Paint from it."

I begin a series of mixed-media paintings, the **Dark Treasure Series.** So far I'm liking the pieces. The first one with a blue slithering dragon winding around a vase, a necklace with a fish floating just above and into the vase. The second one focuses on the large golden vase, with two butterflies, one poised on the front and one wing going off the side of the vase,

and another butterfly flying off to the right and the third, the vase again, but with a dark background and very muted butterflies, misty—kind of like it's disappearing.

Later I go up to Quan Yin and put the necklace, ring and coins in a plastic bag and move the warrior /dragon cap and vase down into my front garden. I leave the prayer flags with Quan Yin.

I go on the Yogichen.org website and search and there I find that in August, September, October and November of last year, many of these vases, at least 60 that I find recorded, were put into the sea off Bodega bay. One entry says, "It was cloudy and cool this morning and the ocean was very calm. We offered 15 vases up to #3711 at Bodega Bay. I slid the money for this month's releasing of lives under Buddha Carlo's door at the Tides Wharf." The Tides, owned by Italian Americans. Owned by "Buddha Carlo."

From the website I find that the YogiChen style of Buddhism is Vajrayana and Mahayana, both of Tibetan and Japanese origin and also practiced on the Malay peninsula. I see pictures of the same man, dressed in an embroidered yellow Chinese style shirt, a baseball cap on his head, with several different couples and families. Each picture is a history of someone's personal grief, a family's loss. They always end up at Bloomfield Cemetery for something to do with the releasing of lives ceremony. Maybe that's where the remains are buried? They release 8 vases one month, 27 one month, 15 one month and so one. Apparently into the three thousands now. On the photo website there is also the same man releasing lives in, where else but Malaysia, home to Burma. Daughter knew somehow.

And I would have to be the one person to find the commemorative vase that beached itself.

My dark treasure from the sea.

I send an email to info@yogichen.org saying I have found one of their butterfly vases and don't know what to do with it and its contents. Unlike Facebook, it takes weeks before I get a comment, much less a "like" or an "unlike." I sit with the dark treasure and await an answer. Finally one comes: "Return it to the sea where it belongs." Yogichen.org has responded. "It's a blessing" is added as an afterthought.

I imagine the next painting I'll make from the vase, from my treasure. Maybe just the delicately black outlined white fish, with a faint triangular shape of an angel fish, and some of the black and white beads. Maybe I'll put in the small circular white ring looking like an albino version of the Buddhist calligraphy circle, the enso. The enso which stands for absolute enlightenment, for the artist becoming one with what he/she creates.

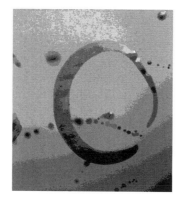

Our Hero Ranger Rick

Here at the West Pole we've lost some of our more practical amenities: the gas station, car repair shop and the bank. Nick Gravenites wrote a song about it: "Since the Gas Station Left Town." In their place, boutiques and yet another restaurant. But no matter how the businesses in town changed, we always had Ranger Rick. That would never change, we assured ourselves.

On a warm late February day, with the ornamental plum trees blooming pink, at the picnic tables in town where Ranger used to sit and relax after pruning, the town hosted a spontaneous memorial. Where he worked crossword puzzles there were mounds of flowers—roses, cala lilies and branches filled with yellow pompom acacia blossoms. Hemp trimmers covered in resin, a bottle of wine, with plastic glasses and a note that said, *Have one for Ranger* sat next to hand-made cards and a large psychedelic mandala with Rick's picture in the center. How, we asked ourselves, will Occidental continue to be, without our Ranger Rick.

Lots of men in town have nicknames; it seems an odd local custom. I didn't even know Ranger's real name, Richard Bruce Kaufman, until I read his obituary. I always thought he was named for that little Raccoon who loved nature—especially frogs and animals in *Ranger Rick Magazine.* I imagined Rick, like the adventurous raccoon, living in the "Deep Green Woods" and for awhile I thought Ranger was a camper, sleeping where he could in the local redwood-covered hills or in a fanciful tree house on someone's acreage. He liked to lecture all of us locals about taking care of the environment. But the real source of his nickname was the "Spaghetti Bowl," a baseball game that went on for years between Camp Meeker and Occidental. Rick would roam the field pounding his mitt, waiting for the ball to come his way. He just ranged around. He was our own Danger Ranger.

Born to a Silicon Valley family, Ranger's father was a scientist, an engineer who died when Rick was still a teenager. Ranger was a buffoon, with a scraggly beard, and wildish graying dark hair covered in a baseball cap in summer, or a warm knit cap in winter. His eyebrows were like Groucho's and his eyes piercing intense pure blue. He could quote philosophers, predict the weather, curse and yelp. He always seemed a very smart guy who gave Yogi Berra type answers to the big questions in life. He came here to live in a commune when he was young and experimented with everything under the sun. He had a family at one time—a wife and two daughters—and was still in touch with his grown daughters and his young grandchildren. He marched to his own particular drummer.

Sometimes he'd yell and swear, a sign he was off the wagon or into LSD, but he could tell you if a big storm was coming in or what the stars and planets were up to in the heavens. It's a perspective I fully appreciated. He was Shakespearian—a fool, a trickster, a truth teller. He pruned all the trees and kept the flowering quinces looking good. He scolded kids and adults who created clutter and locals who had "attitude problems."

He was the king character in a town full of characters. It's my town and I guess I'm a character too, but not nearly as noteworthy as Ranger Rick.

When I've had a rare public squabble with someone, maybe I don't want to say it, but could be my husband, Rick irritated me because he chimed in—usually on the side of the hubby. "Quit yer belly aching." "Let the man talk." and once at a memorial downtown for a local man who committed suicide because he just couldn't stand to be in pain any longer, Rick interrupted the speeches with hoots and howls. Some how the whole thing seemed funny and infuriating to him at the same time. I think it was his particular way to deal with his own grief. He liked the guy. We tried to shush him up, but then just accepted his growls and comments and laughs as part of the ceremony.

Usually Rick was in jeans and a long sleeved shirt, or in the heat a pretty scruffy tee shirt. Sometimes in winter he wore overalls or a big jacket. Or a big gray sweatshirt, tennis shoes and his cap. He often showed up unannounced to sit quietly at a literary reading or at a music event. When there was a street band playing, he'd be out there dancing with the best of them. A fast taskmaster, twirling you all over the place on purpose to see if he could trick you or make you dizzy, make you laugh. It seemed right on the edge of hostility sometimes.

Ranger Rick was nice to kids and lovely local women. He'd bow taking off his little baseball cap.

He was paid by the town to do the clean up and he sometimes got a free meal as part of the deal. He was often 86'd from the bars in town. He was helped by a local dentist and the paella maker to get a new set of teeth through a special program, and finally didn't cover his mouth when he talked or smiled. I had no idea his teeth were a big mess and always hurting him. When you don't have money it's hard to take care of your teeth. Shortly after this my old wine barrel house landlady cleaned him up, rented him a tux, and he was her date at a local fund-raising dance. Maybe it took him back to high school, where he was an honor student, maybe to his marriage, or maybe he just enjoyed being ever unpredictably lovable.

The last time I saw him he had lodgings on a tree-filled piece of property near the cemetery where he's now buried. He needed a ride home—it was dark, after the Super Bowl was over. "Sure, hop in."

"Nice car, what is it?"

"New Honda CRV," I said. "The kids tell me it's my last car." He laughed.

"I gave my old car to Rowan and her husband who have just had fraternal twin boys, three months early, but now the boys are home and everything is okay."

"Nice, great!" he said.

"Beautiful place I have here now," he said. "The guy's trading me this cabin for work around the property." He seemed pleased with his luck. He was clear and sweet on this last time I ever saw him. He died in his sleep just a few days later in this little cabin on the hillside, of "acute alcoholic induced liver failure," it said in the paper. He had his demons.

Rick always had something to say. Strong political opinions and harsh comments about tourists who don't do things according to Occidental's unspoken rules, like pick up after yourself and be friendly, and don't just ignore him or anyone, for that matter. And park straight, and look a little funky.

There was a memorial for him at the red-steepled Catholic church and his family and the town—more than 400 people attended and spoke. Then we gathered at one of the Italian restaurants after. We had to let him go. It was like saying goodbye to a kind of crazy uncle, or a prophetic fool, there was something about his free spirit, his irascible nature, his quips and digs, that had touched us.

"Why is all this here and who was he?" my seven-year old granddaughter asked as we walked by the impromptu memorial.

It's kind of hard to explain and I'm amazed they didn't notice Ranger Rick, but they don't know who he was. Not quite old enough for him to poke at them with his irreverence. He did, after all have a complete soft spot for little kids.

Sometimes he was a nuisance, sometimes a philosopher, sometimes an ordinary drunken lout, but always, he was himself, predictably colorful and outspoken, the fool in a town of fools. I will miss him. He was one of a kind, part of our big West County extended family. I am always sure I'll see him as I turn that last bend into town. He just has to be there.

And so he is, small and made of metal, almost on top of a green metal trash bin, but there he is. Ranger Rick as immortalized forever by artist Patrick Amiot.

Snakeskin

Paper thin
in the hand
soft as a fledgling's
feather.
Purpose over—
done with it.
Like getting out of
a pair of nylons,
too tight jeans—
requires wriggling around
sometimes on the floor.
Snakeskin boots
purses.
Discarded
on the path—
Snakeskin.

Shedding My Skin

Sonoma County, California, is diamond-back rattlesnake territory. They're abundant and venomous. They love the golden grasses and rock outcrops and abundance of small rodents and insects. I've seen them where I live on Fiori Lane and I heard that two years ago they killed a neighbor's furry black dog, Jack, with a bite. They are moving in from the hills to our countrified neighborhoods.

My friend Joe was bitten by a rattler when he retrieved a volleyball during a game. For months after, his leg was a purple, mottled mess. I think he kind of liked to show it to people because it always got a rise. In a way, it was his badge of survival, maybe even bravery. I was shocked when I saw his leg and wondered if it would ever return to normal. Those of us who saw Joe's leg were all probably thinking the same thing—it could, easily happen to us.

Our friend Micah was also bitten by a rattler. He was just walking out to his mailbox. My friend Davis was struck when she went out on her deck to see what her dog was fussing about. The cornered snake didn't even warn Davis, simply struck on a balmy summer night. She was an easy target in her flimsy pajamas. She stayed at Kaiser Hospital for days, feverish and occasionally delirious. All three of these snake-bitten friends survived to tell their snake tales.

A friend from South Africa told me he had to run as fast as he could to outrun a racing African Black Mamba snake. Sometimes it feels like I'm trying to outrun some of my memories. They seem to be keeping pace beside me these days, trying for a bite—trying to drag me down and stick their fangs into me.

Snakes use their venom to paralyze or kill prey. In the natural world enemies often warn their prey with a coloration or a warning sound. It only seems fair that a snake should hiss, or in the case of the venomous rattler, shake its rattles to tell you: Stay Away! My grandchildren love to pick rattlesnake grass and shake it to make it rattle, and then strip off the rattles—projectiles designed by nature to fly off and dig into the ground. But I've warned about real snakes and said, "No matter what, don't pick up a snake, and don't get too close. If it rattles at you, quietly and slowly back away." They are waiting to see one. It sounds exciting to them.

Sadira's told me many times, "We won't, Gramma, but we really really want to see one."

I worry that they will pick up a snake. My older grandson, Sky, does pick up snakes. But he says he knows the safe ones, the racers, garter and gopher snakes. And he knows how to grab them so they won't bite. Or try to.

My dad taught me how to use a shovel to behead a rattler. He lived in a valley loaded with the snakes, and felt they were dangerous, lurking in the wood piles. Still, I've never wanted to harm one. I figure to just keep my distance and I'll be fine. If they were about to strike one of my grandchildren though, I wouldn't hesitate to use a shovel.

In Chinese astrology I'm born in the year of the snake and when I catch myself in a mirror, I notice that my blue-grey eyes look like snakes eyes, with little pupils and an intent stare. Snakes have no eyelids, so they seem to stare, glare almost. The Chinese horoscope says about those of us born in 1941: "The snake is clever, cunning, intelligent, and endures great hardships: it's unforgiving and power hungry." I don't see myself as interested in control, but maybe I can be a little on the cunning side.

Last week I stopped by my friend Betty Ann's antique store.

"How do you feel about snakes?" she asks me. "I'm fascinated by them," I say.

"We've got one in the store. Do you think you can coax it out?" I walk in and look where she pointing. "Oh it's just a little garter snake," I say. "It's scared so it's all curled up in a corner under the old pie safe. Hmmm, do you have something flat, like a shovel or a dust pan?" I ask her. "I need a broom too." "Oh," she says, "never mind, I'm going next door to the Gallery to see if Rik is there." "Mylette's there." I say. "Oh, man, she doesn't like snakes," Betty Ann says, "I'm going to call Rik at his home."

I guess Betty Ann doesn't trust me with a snake even though in Chinese Astrology I am a snake. She thinks I'll squeal and run for it when the snake wriggles. And I might. After lunch I stop back by and there's Rik. He's the hero. He first tried my approach which was to broom the snake into a dust pan, like it was a pile of broken glass, but the snake dove for it. Jumped right off the dustpan and scooted away. The broom approach worked though. Snake, encouraged by straw bristle, went out the back door and slithered into the gallery garden next door. I tell Mylette. She says, "I hate snakes. I guess I won't water out there today."

Snakes have gotten a lot of bad press. There's that story of Adam and Eve with that seductive snake—sneaky and trying to get Eve into trouble with God. But, like a lot of creatures, they have a place and purpose in the food chain. They devour rodents. Since there are millions of gophers where we live, some people have been buying gopher snakes to route out the pesky rodents. I see more and more gopher snakes in our neighborhood, and on walks. Trouble is, from a distance I can't really tell them apart from a rattler. Their markings are similar, and they fake a rattle by banging their tail on the ground.

Honestly, it's the quietness of snakes that unnerves me. In the garden I come across them gliding over the rough red brick path into the salvias, or sometimes sunning themselves at the top of the driveway—drawn to the warmth of asphalt.

But I'm drawn to discarded snakeskins. I can't help picking up and inspecting the paper thin bits of skin. Delicate and so very soft. Like a silk sweater, it looks like it was knit on a very fine hand-loom. Sometimes the powdery skin just dis-integrates in my sweaty gardener's hands. One of my grand-sons collects lizard's discarded skins, but he has yet to find an intact snakeskin.

There are memories I'd like to outrun and out-distance myself from like my friend did with the Black Mamba, but still they crop up to haunt me, like the wispy snake skins I love to find.

In my 70s now, I feel like what I'm doing is shedding my skin—discarding parts of my past, and squeezing into what is to become old age. My new snake skin will be tougher, and its pattern will warn away any predators. My old skin will be left lying in the sun somewhere for a small boy or an old woman to find.

Missing Time

The Unicorn Room buried a time capsule in 1981 on the property of one of Mary Lea's Harmony School classmates, Chad. Thirty years later I live across the street from Chad, his wife and two kids. It's not really a street, more of a lane where the phantom time capsule lies in wait for an unveiling later this summer. There's a big problem, though—the time capsule's gone missing. Harmony School's Unicorn Room's treasures are not to be found. They've done a Unicorn thing and vanished.

Chad's parents got divorced and neither parent can find the map to the time capsule. Harmony School was given a copy of the map at the time of the interment, but since then, the school moved from downtown Occidental into the redwoods in Freestone. The school has no record of the map. Chad has scoured his family home and looked in the school's two safes. Still, no map to buried treasure.

Chad describes the time capsule as an emptied-out green plastic pickle barrel ample enough for a stash of the Unicorn Room's treasures from the early eighties, an odd and eclectic assortment to show what it was like in 1981 for kids. Or at least what the kids from the combination 4th-5th-6th grade in western Sonoma County thought might be fun to see again. Stuff they thought was important.

As he remembers it, the most desirable item in the capsule is a hand-held "Simon" electronic game. *Hello Kitty* was big at the time, and there is at least one *Hello Kitty* purse. Mary Lea remembers nail polish and a photo of Michael Jackson. She thinks there might also be a hand-made "god's eye," colorful yarn woven around two small redwood twigs in a diamond shape. Important things of no consequence. Something from every kid in the Unicorn Room to evoke a certain time. Not sure if there's a unicorn in there or not. Maybe someone put in a dream catcher, another hand-woven piece of art that captures your dreams at night and keeps you safe from nightmares.

Are these buried treasures waiting quietly in the dark, fertile acid soil of west Sonoma County, or gone? The apple trees on the time capsule property are gone, replaced by loads of scraggly madrones, acacias, and coyote brush. The property is still framed though, as in 1981, by 200-year-old eucalyptus trees and massive redwoods. Chad first had to dig out mounds of poison oak, and blackberry bushes planted by his parents and thriving in their native environment. He's followed his dad's instructions on where he remembers the time capsule being buried—towards the edge of the property adjacent to the road. Chad tried a metal detector, nothing. He tried a post hole digger and hired a backhoe trencher. Nothing. Finally he spent a bunch of money on a "ground penetrating radar specialist." No green plastic barrel, no *Hello Kitty* purse, no dream catcher. Maybe it was raided by gophers lusting after the Aquafresh striped toothpaste and the Coca Cola that are also in the capsule.

Chad made a Facebook group for the Unicorn Room Time Capsule. Mary Lea hasn't joined yet, she's not on Facebook. She has two little kids, ages 6 and 7, to mind. There is supposed to be a big party, on the same day I'm having one to celebrate my 70th birthday. But the capsule party may not happen now, or the group may still get together on the time capsule property to celebrate anyway.

On Facebook, members of the Unicorn Room Time Capsule share memories of where it was buried: "Near the road near some apple trees." Someone else adds, "The apple trees are gone now." Every suggestion has been noted and checked out, but sites and people's memories alter over thirty years. Many people suggest the large gopher theory and one mother thinks maybe the time capsule has already been dug up.

In 2011, Mary Lea's and Chad's children go to the new improved version of Harmony School on a beautiful site with an Environmental Center and a garden where the kids grow some of the food for their lunches. They study the life cycle of salmon in Salmon Creek which cuts through the Bohemian Highway side of the campus. The classes are smaller than in the day of the Unicorn Room and the parents include some nuevo hippies, some into the "soccer mom" era, some organic farmers, some multi-generational Italian families. A similar mix to what the school has always been. The kids still go to school in portables, but they are prettier portables, and probably more earthquake proof than in the day when my kids were little.

Each time I walk my dog down Fiori Lane, with clumps of naked ladies in full bloom this mid-August time of the year, I check on Chad's progress. The cleared and scraped area shows so many random and mistaken digs that the property looks like something from the movie *Holes*. Each hole with a little wire and bit of orange material fluttering from it, like a small flag marking each spot. Sort of a "been there" marker. But still, it's no go. Nothing found yet—not in that ground. As the days go by, on my walks I see yet more holes, more bright flags, but no green pickle barrel treasures placed carefully by a bunch of enthusiastic nine, ten, and eleven-year-olds at Harmony School.

Chad said there were copies of the *Unicorn News* in the capsule. The news was first written by his mom Carol, and then later, and not as cleverly, by me. The *Unicorn News* caught the parents up with what was going on in the classroom, and what field trips were coming up, what special events, and it was done in a very readable and humorous way. The kids contributed to it and the teacher, Phylis Osborne did too. Everyone from the Unicorn Room loved to read the news.

The year 1981 was the time of *Raiders of the Lost Ark*, Ronald Reagan, the wedding of Prince Charles to the beautiful Lady Diana. This was when the first home computers were making inroads and the beginnings of MTV. It was when Mary Lea and her friend Shana were writing to Michael Jackson with their fan loyalty and sending him a recording of them singing a song to him that they had written especially for him. "We love you, Michael," they said at the end, practically in tears. Posters of Michael were plastered all over Mary Lea's room. I was in Western Ireland when Michael Jackson died two years ago and the Irish were grief stricken. Mary Lea not so much. The singer and pop idol had changed and so had she.

But in 1981 she was mad at me. "You just don't understand, Mom, how much I do love him." She was right, I'd forgotten my own intense crushes on Elvis and later on Ricky Nelson.

Blondie was also popular, but I wouldn't let Mary Lea listen to her, even though her older sister in the next room was listening. The Unicorn Room was happening at the same time the first "test tube baby" was being born. Cabbage Patch dolls were still an item and in 1981 I had my own version of one: a one-year-old curly-haired toddler slung against my hip at all the parent meetings at the school.

Time marches on. All the Unicorn Room children are middle-aged now, 40 years old or older. They mostly have kids of their own, and a lot of them still live in the area. But some are coming from far away, from the east coast, just to celebrate the time capsule non-opening. They might just have a barbecue and go swimming, Mary Lea tells me. She might have to come late to my party. She has, after all, "waited thirty years for this." My party is at the new arts center, in the old Harmony School, so it's all strung together by community memories, sort of a mythological high wire dance done over the years. The daughter in the room listening to Blondie teaches English on the Central Coast, her son turning 13 next month. The Cabbage Patch baby is pregnant with twins of her own.

Folks in the Facebook group, The Unicorn Room Time Capsule, are telling Chad that in a way they've already opened the time capsule by reconnecting via the popular social media of 2011. They've been sharing memories and telling about their lives now. Still, it might be fun to look at some old headlines and see a few issues of the *Unicorn News*—even if they might have a little mold clinging to the pages.

Time—it's always lost anyway. Every minute of every day is ticking away. I am about to turn 70 this summer of 2011. It's an age that finally, really feels old to me—the number is scary, even though I don't feel old and still have plenty of energy and decent health—at least as good or better than it's always been. Still, people are starting to treat me a little differently. My hair is mostly all white in front. I'm part of a big avalanche of boomers and pre-boomers. We're marked by that snowy hair.

I plan to dance though, at my party, and the tunes, from the 60's on up, will kick in memories of my own. A sort of inner time capsule.

Dangers of Dancing

Dancing
quiet danger,
unspoken fears,
arms just so,
you miss a beat
misstep,
tangled feet.

Like picking up
a sharpened
kitchen knife
edge faces away
handle rough grip
when carving
don't slip.

Like opening
the ink bottle,
dark liquid
not to be erased
take time when
you make
the letter O,
it's forever.

Cut into
a browned bird
lines appear
dinner line forms
slit in pan
can catch
the juices.

Glide
across
the floor,
dip your partner
low. She
smiles, her mouth
like a bow.

Don the Dancer from Two Guys
with a Big Truck

In the fury of winter our little black metal Squirrel wood-stove chatters away, burning perfectly cylindrical logs and warming us. With a wood box too small for most regular firewood, compressed logs are the right snug fit. They burn slowly, so that only one of us has to ease out from under the down comforter in the cold night to throw on another log and then crank the Squirrel's air vents down tight.

From our bedroom we hear the soft hum of a small cordless fan as it whirs away on top of the stove, the coil on the bottom of the fan growing hotter along with the fire, making the blades whirl faster and faster. If you stand right in front of the wood-stove you don't feel much heat, but after a while the fan pushes the warmth out into the room so that soon the air is cozily warm. In my reading chair I pull off a favorite bunched-up sweater, full of small insistent burrs, toss off well-worn Ugg boots lined with once-white lamb's wool, pick up a book and settle comfortably into winter.

For 15 years we've bought pressed logs from Two Guys with a Big Truck. Except the name's not right now; there's only one guy to wrestle the big old truck, tilting and creaking, brakes squealing, backing down our steep driveway. Don, the one guy, arrives with the stacked pallet top-knotted with greenery—mostly red bottle brushes from the trees the truck has had to duck under. The one guy Don pushes a lever which lowers the tail gate, delivering the stack along with a fork lift onto our drive. He hops onto the lift and picks off the load—round and square at the same time. The pallet of logs is covered in plastic so the logs won't get wet and revert back to what they were—sawdust from a lumber mill. Don carefully maneuvers the load into place and lowers it on the driveway. That's when my husband appears, gloves on, wheelbarrow at the ready to put all the logs away inside boxes specifically designed and built to fit the logs. My husband Forrest is an exacting type, a mathematician, and he wants life managed.

When I first met the one guy, I was wary of him. He seemed crotchety and grizzled, with a scraggly beard. He wore a knit cap to cover unkempt hair.

"Vietnam vet," he'd always announce as soon as he'd climb down from his high truck seat to unstrap the pallet of wood. It was almost as though being a Vietnam vet defined him. Tough, perhaps bitter, it weighed him down until he was a huge man protected by his own layers. He'd tug on his ruffled beard hairs as he snapped at me, snarled at the dog, "Get out of the way, girl." I never knew if he meant me or the dog—probably both. "Don's the name," he'd remind me as he turned to leave. He'd noisily rumble back up the drive, shifting rusty gears and barely making it out the top.

When we moved to our current home, with its similarly steep driveway and our newly purchased Morsø Squirrel wood-stove, Don had a transformation. A metamorphosis took place.

He lost weight and trimmed his beard and was kind of friend-ly. He even laughed.

"Don, you look great," I said to him on one delivery day, "What's your secret?"

Barely looking at me as he carefully pressed the levers of his loader, speaking in a soft voice, the word "dancing" tumbled out of the down-turned corners of his mouth. "Ballroom dancing. I never danced as a young guy, but turns out I'm good at it."

I knew what he'd been doing as a young guy—crawling through tunnels in Vietnam.

"Dancing. That is something I wish my husband would take up with me."

His caterpillar's transformation has held steady. He's stayed thin, trimmed up and seems happy. Sometimes he talks about life on the Russian River, about how his wife's jewelry business is thriving. She doesn't dance, but he still loves to dance and she doesn't mind his dancing with multiple partners.

Recently he was backing down the driveway as I was try-ing to drive up. We did a sort of automotive dance of our own until we both ended up where we needed to be. I asked out the window of my car, "How's the dancer?"

" Oh," he said, eyes fiery, grin wide and true, "I had a break-through, a real breakthrough. My teacher told me that I step on my dance partner's feet because I don't feel where her feet are in my frame. I feel her hips, hold her arms and hands, but her feet in my frame? I didn't get it at first. And then I did. It makes all the difference now."

I consider telling him that he's had an epiphany of intu-ition. That now he's a more tuned-in guy, a one Zen moment guy, but I just smile, and wave as I drive away.

Later that night as I sit sipping wine by the Squirrel with her glow of coals and steady flicker of flame. My mind wan-ders back to Don.

I like to imagine that he has left the tunnels of Vietnam far behind as he twirls, feet flying, knowing exactly where his lady will place the toes of her dancing shoes, sensing just where her heel will land as his foot clicks up behind him. I can see that he probably dances as deftly and gently as he guides that chunky pallet of wood in between the dusty chalk lines my husband has scratched onto the driveway to show Don exactly where the wood should go. And if I'm lucky, I think, someday my husband will also resemble a butterfly with his dancing shoes polished, his mind set on the next move.

Musical Milagritos in the Redwoods

My eyes are on the violin player. How she swiftly and exactingly draws her bow across her shiny small wooden instrument, chin tucked loosely into its chin rest. I'm always stunned at how these skilled musicians can draw me into their sounds, their galloping music, to pull an emotion from me as they go.

In 1980 two local women had an idea to create an arts organization to bring quartet and other classical music to a small intimate environment in Occidental, and it has worked for over 30 years. Kit Neustadter and Janet Greene founded the Redwood Arts Council. Then along came Doris Murphy, who decided the RAC and the local Occidental Community Choir needed a permanent home. These three women, along with a flood of dedicated volunteers helped bring culture to the West Pole.

Kit, in particular created a lasting tribute to her dedication. She was not a musician but grew up listening to live musicians play in her father's and stepmother's home, reluctantly at first, until she got hooked. The organization's coordinator, now that Kit has passed away, is someone youngish and vital and full of love for fine classical performances.

I came to the very first concert, a harpsichord recital by Janet Greene, the other original founder of the Redwood Arts Council. She dropped out after a few years, but now acts as an advisor to the new arts center. And she still teaches Orff music lessons to local children, just as she taught Mary Lea and Rowan when they were in elementary school.

At first the music concerts were held in the two local churches. The "red church" which is Catholic, and the "white church," a protestant church. Eventually the white church hosted the majority of the performances. Musicians said the acoustics in what is basically a wooden box, were incredible.

In those early years I came with Scott, and we sat on uncomfortable church pews looking up at signs that said: *He is Risen,* and *Come unto me.* A Christian god listening to secular music along with the rest of us

The Redwood Arts Council has hosted The Kronos Quartet, John Hammond on his steel guitar, the Alexander String Quartet, a delicate Cambodian shadow puppet play, and a retelling of Dylan Thomas's "A Child's Christmas in Wales," with Celtic harp. One early concert featured original instruments made by the husband of the kids' school teacher. He used water and pipes to make sounds. Very different, fun, and impressive. Science and art combine in the world of music.

We've seen Baroque instruments packed for travel, elaborately hand-painted harpsichords and dark grand pianos carefully set into place and tuned. We've heard brass ensembles, gospel groups and *Kitka* singing acapella music from Eastern Europe. These groups, a saving grace to me, have been a kind of *milagrito,* a "little miracle." When I moved here at age 36 I wondered how I would ever survive winters 60 miles away from the cultural hub of San Francisco.

Sometimes, when the concerts were in the "white church," you could hear Ranger Rick yelling through the windows. But other times he would quietly sit in the back listening for a while, if there was room for him. Before the Occidental Center for the Arts became a reality in what used to be our town's elementary school, at intermission we'd line up in the church kitchens to buy cookies, cocoa, tea, coffee, and CDs from the evening's musicians. There was always a second line leading to the bathroom just around the corner from the kitchen, where we could hear the musicians tuning up right through the wall. Now they have a full-fledged green room at the new center, but sometimes still, you can hear them tuning up. I don't mind. I think of how they've traveled to get here: planes, cars, buses, long distances. Their instruments with them the whole way, unless they're piano players.

In those days of music in the churches, every once in a while, I noticed that guy Forrest I'd met in Occidental, and see his name listed in the program as a donor to the organization. I'd never thought of him as the type, a "long-hair," as we used to say, who might enjoy classical music. But some 30 years later, here he is at my side, hands folded and relaxing into music. Touched by it, even, because at the end I see him surreptitiously wipe away a tear. He is a guy who loves music, but has never tried to play an instrument. I saw him play bongo drums once years ago at a party, when he gave me a long glance, a look of a man eager to find love. He was on the beat, but it wasn't his musical stylings that won my heart. He has no innate sense of music and a tin ear, so he can't carry a tune. What impressed me was seeing him at these concerts, knowing that he put his money behind them, and that he was trying to as he said one time, "broaden" his musical knowledge. Unlike me, he hadn't been exposed to much classical music as a kid. His dad listened to the big band sound of Glen Miller, but that was it. He is a student of everything, with an immense curiousity about the world, and now that includes all the arts.

This drizzly evening we arrive at the Occidental Center for the Arts, a solid reality now, a cultural fixture on our landscape. We take the last two seats left. We're pleased to see it's a full house for these talented young players of the Chiara String

Quartet who've brought their violins, cello and viola from Nebraska. The second violinist also has her small breastfeeding daughter with her on the trip, babysat tonight, she tells me at the reception following the concert, by a cousin from the Bay Area.

The Chiara Quartet plays two different works by Beethoven, very demanding, energetic pieces. The early one, before Beethoven became completely deaf, is much more lively and leaping than the later one—which seems deep and darker—but both pieces are athletic feats of skill for the musicians. They are sweaty in the overly hot, semi-professional lighting of the OCA, with dots of perspiration, like small jewels shining on their faces. In between the Beethoven pieces, they perform a striking new piece written specifically for them by Gabriela Lena Frank, born in 1972, a year after my musically-talented daughter Mary Lea. The name of the piece: *Milagros*.

Hot off the composer's music sheets, written this year, 2010, each of the eight movements are called *Milagritos*, with lovely Spanish names like *Capilla del Camino* (Shrine by the Road) and *Zamponas Rotas* (Broken Panpipes). The young composer was inspired by what she's seen and heard traveling in her mother's homeland, Peru. Gabriela explains in the liner notes that while the movements are inspired by ordinary daily Peruvian events, to her they seem "quietly miraculous."

Shrines by the road. As this movement opens, I think of the ones I've seen for those who've died in accidents. I would construct a Mexican roadside shrine for my brother, if only I knew exactly where on the road he died between Tijuana and Ensenada when he was 19 years old. I try my best to leave this harsh old memory and enter into the music. I am soothed by music, I know it will take me away from this scarred-over wound of loss and transport me to another world.

Soon I'm mesmerized by the relentless Latin rhythm of the piece, and the way the bows curve across the instruments, how strong, nimble fingers pluck at the strings, pizzicato style.

The group gets a standing ovation. My hands sting from clapping as hard as I can until it drives the tears from my eyes. I hate to cry in front of people, but I'm moved by the music, and, well, a lot of different things this evening. Forrest looks at me and gives me a smile. He puts his arm around me and gives me a squeeze.

At the reception following, I thank the musicians for coming all the way out to our small rural town to perform for us, and the cello player says, "Occidental is charming! The people are so friendly, and the redwoods so amazingly beautiful."

"It's what we do; we can't always do big venues," the viola player adds.

I think our grandkids may soon be ready to sit through at least a half concert, like some of the other children I see. Musicians in the making need to see performances and hear music they don't usually have access to at school or even at home. Skyler plays guitar and piano, Sadira the saxophone, and this year Saben Jr. will take up some instrument, he thinks the drums. The twins just rock out to music, bending their toddler knees and attempting to snap their fingers. I think it's great exposure for every child to hear and see concerts with traditional music and instruments. As we drive back through the woods to home, I think about the miracle of music and the people who have the gift and drive to compose it or to create it.

I say a silent thank you to Kit, to Doris and to Janet, and to all the community volunteers who help make this musical interlude possible. I know the next time I sit at the arts center I'll be listening to the Occidental Community Choir with Mary Lea and Scott up there singing, "Music from Home," and I'll have a big lump in my throat. And then, when members of the choir walk out into the hall and surround the audience, I'll be singing along with them:

"Music from home, sing me a true song. Music from home, one of your own. Music from home, when I'm lonely, I need music, music from home."

Dappled Man

In the fall's changing light,
in the dark dappled green-treed afternoon,
a man lies dying in his deep forest home.
Wife and daughters comfort him,
cluster at his side while birds swoop low
over the silvered smoking stove pipe outside,
fly down, landing on his grayed hospital bed.

He lies surrounded by blackbirds,
beaks tucked tightly under their wings.

He lies in the living room next to rows of cans
filled with rusty nails of every size.
They spill out across the bamboo floor
like a game of pick-up-sticks,
like redwood duff tossed on a high wind.
How to put it right? he wonders aloud.

The house, once caught up with pink sunsets
and pink daughters peering out of windows
double glazed against winter
now holds flocks of feathered spectators,
though there is no long-fluted birdsong.

His doctor stops whistling like a bird
and takes a seat to wait while

wings tipped in black, dipped in death
spread across the man's body at his nested home.

His voice, still strong, booms out,
"I need finish nails.
Go fetch me some nails! And a hammer too."
He swings his arm in an arc,
driving in nails, finishing what has not been.

"Time has arranged against me,"
he shouts to no one in particular.
His wife and daughters look at each other.
They frown, but don't leave his side.

"I must blow my trumpet to shake the trees,
wake the hills, all the way down
to the chapeled town, the gray-whaled sea."

At last he sleeps.
He sleeps, but more like a cat naps.
He imagines making a huge furred leap
into the treetops and leaving his dreams there like scat.

He waits for a cloud shaped like a hammer, or a heron,
he can't decide which, before he can wake again.
His phantom feet only graze the shadows
in the dappled green-treed afternoon.

RIP Steve Steen-Larsen 2012

Trouble in Paradise

This year makes 36 years living at the West Pole. It's familiar terrain now, home sweet home. But not all is sweetness, light or happy endings. People get older, I'm 72 now, my "kids" mostly middle-aged. My first husband is dead, my second just remarried. and Forrest has heart issues. Still we live in paradise. We tell ourselves that every night when we shut out the lights, knowing that if we stepped outside we'd clearly see the constellations, or a big bright harvest moon, which often ends up shining into our bedroom through the gauzy Indian curtains block-printed in turquoise and lime green.

We think of ourselves as insulated here in paradise. If we never listened to the news or read a newspaper, we would just wake up and see the redwood trees, hear the jays squawking about their territory and watch male hummingbirds doing their fly-bys to impress the females, first climbing straight up into the blue and then making a sort of super sonic whistle as they dive down.

We hear the occasional dog bark, coyote howl or fox yip, but don't think of terrorists or economic woes, or the continual bickering of political candidates. This time of the year, in early fall, we pick our over-abundant zucchini, and fret that the tomatoes are taking forever to get ripe because it's been a foggy summer.

Except that our friends are dying of cancer, or have just been diagnosed with cancer. The two stalwarts of the Italian restaurant families, young men, both dead from cancer. What is it with the cancer thing? Here we are the granola generation dedicated to healthy foods and life out in nature, and still cells go bad and multiply. It just doesn't seem right. Of course as kids we ate junk and we endured drift floating into California from the Neveda desert A-bomb test sites, and we women were the first to take the strong hormones of the Pill.

As my brother says, "We are next in line." Or as my children say: "The old ones have to leave to make room for the babies." We are lucky to see babies all around us. Billions of people on the planet and more on the way every day, more arriving than leaving.

Some friends are dying due to simple failure of aged body parts, like in the case of our 101-year-old friend Doris, who had a vision of an Arts Center which has come true. Her legacy. And lots of old parents are going. Ours lost to us for years now.

Or there are the tragic times in our small town, like in big towns, when kids have killed themselves or died in accidents. So the misplaced sense of security and beauty and the feeling, perhaps fanciful, that all is well with the universe is just that—a fantasy. Maybe we don't live in Brigadoon afterall. We're like everyone else, but maybe without such extremes as planes flying into buildings in our neighborhood, or dead people showing up on our lawns. We mostly don't have lawns, and any dead bodies that are left lying about are probably very efficiently dealt with by turkey vultures or other scavengers.

We haven't had to clean up an entire neighborhood after a hurricane like in New York and New Orleans, but occasionally the nearby Russian River floods and people have to shovel muck out of the lower part of their houses or out of their businesses. Sometimes trees fall, breaking through rooftops or damaging lines and causing power outages. And just last week my daughter Mary Lea called to ask if the whole family could come over to our house for the night. A home two doors down from her in the trees of Camp Meeker was on fire, raging, crackling. Her husband posted a frightening video of it on Facebook. Later she called back to say the volunteer firefighters had put the fire out, contained it, but the house itself, dating back almost two hundred years was only a mass of charred timbers. We live in a fire ravaged state.

My art patron, a writer who hired me to do illustrations for his books, died on the East Coast at his first home. Then a friend who writes poetry, a larger than life woman with coal-colored hair and a dose of largesse went out. At her memorial a flute and a harpsichord were played—the music she loved. Her son read some of her quirky, entertaining poetry. A friend drowned in a third world country. And most recently one friend died of diabetes and three more succumbed to cancer. It's not easy to watch someone waste away. It's almost a relief when the end comes for them, even though it doesn't stop grief from striking—lashing out. Already one husband has quickly coupled up with a new wife, and another has found true love, number two, but the others left behind are still trying to redefine themselves without being a half of a couple anymore.

It's also been a year of separations and divorces. Old people in their 60's and 70's giving up on relationships, or in the case of two couples, an old man finding a much younger woman in a third world country. The last gasp, "the fourth quarter," as a friend tried to rationalize this wild billy goat behavior. Men love football metaphors.

To me it seems the same old story, lust, a fear of mortality, but the rawness and closeness keeps me awake at night. Pain in all its recognizable forms. And imagining the happiness and relief that can also come with divorce and a new love. The familiar irritations gone, but without them, perhaps a longing for the familiar. Like a new tender skin that grows over a wound, when you touch it, it still hurts. And the new is not always as pleasant, not so Cinderella-esque as imagined.

But the wife left for the new young one, found a new guy, a perhaps even better guy. We all just attended the beautiful hopeful wedding of my ex, Scott. New family members for our children, and his too, new step-siblings. Bigger is better I think.

For the really sad events there are a few feel good things one can do. Making meals is always a good thing, or adding a sage-wrapped log to a bonfire helps a little. Or taking a friend to a sad sad cathartic movie—*Les Miserables* for example. A few times I've just busted down sobbing in the middle of the night. All is change but change can be unwelcome.

Looking through old photographs gives the true sense of time passing as dark hair lightens into white or gray, babies stretch into gawky teenagers, kids turn into parents. I've thought it might be fun to make a kaleidoscope full of cut up, collaged faces. As you turn the eye piece multiple layers turn the faces into patterns; it would be as beautiful, as the colored glass shapes I see when I play with my grandchildren's kaleidoscope.

This time of life has brought a welcomed transformation to my husband, Forrest. With the threat of possible heart surgery hanging over him he's embraced exercise, and while not giving up totally on pastries and carbohydrates, he has changed his diet and lost over 35 pounds, with a goal to lose another 30. After turning down my offers to "take a walk" for over 25 years, he is finally holding out his hand to me and offering ideas about where we might trudge up and down hills. While there is a certain bittersweet quality to this, I'm relieved and gratefully accept and treasure the sharing of a walk together. He of course brings along his pedometer, to keep track of exactly how many cardio rate steps we take while I drift along looking for hawks.

We are losing our hearing—blame it on all those rock concerts. We are all losing our memories—I like to say that the computer in my head is too full, like a big filing cabinet with random loose papers poking out from the drawers. I'm slow to remember acquaintances names and faces resulting in moments of humor, or sometimes embarrassment. But I accept it all as a trade off for still being here, still in this place I've loved for 36 years, and the places I loved but stepped away from, before that.

I have a new car. "Probably your last one," my daughters point out. Time is more finite now.

The dream house built with Scott when we first moved to the West Pole was purchased by friends during our divorce. The house did not make us whole after all, but this next couple and their children have lived there for more than 25 years. I've loved seeing the changes and improvements these friends made to the place over the years.

Marie and Joe, a couple we used to sip beers with at the Union Hotel while listening to accordion music as our kids danced around are still together after 40 years. But a tragedy took place near their vacation home and everyone is trying to recover from our friend's death in the ocean there. The shock of it has strained the strings that bind this old group of friends together. Still the women friends I've made here and had for 36 years still provide solace for each other and in our older years we refer to ourselves as The Dueñas. We've raised families together and seen each other through the hard times as well as many fun times.

Ranger Rick no longer sweeps up, gardens, curses and sings. Somehow it's so much quieter without him, but the place is messier, the plants untended, and the young people at the local taverns more out of control. If Rick were around, he'd yell at them and they'd listen.

At the West Pole there are new generations and we see more baby strollers at the Friday Farmers Markets. Young families everywhere. Nuevo hippies and hipsters and ordinary families meeting their neighbors at the market and buying whatever veggies they don't have growing in their own gardens. They eat paella, or buy brick oven baked pizzas to share with their kids.

Maybe, as my sister says, the magnetic pole has already shifted and our planet has begun its increased wobble. She says no one wants us to panic, so we haven't been told yet. Magnetic wobble is one of the explanations given for the end of the Mayan Calendar in 2012. But we feel the shift, even if we don't know it for sure; because everyone seems in a whirl. The West Pole may be slightly less to the west; maybe it's shifting toward the center of the earth after all.

At my memorial service let someone play a bit from a Brahms trio, the cello deep and moody, the clarinet flitting above, light and melodic. Maybe there could be some funny stories told; I've had my share of misadventures. Don't ask my children or grandchildren to sing or speak, unless they really really want to. Make the service short and have pictures and most of all, good things to eat and drink.

And if you can, please arrange for an accordionist to come and play lively tunes, like the ones we listened to in the Union Hotel bar when we first came to this West Pole. I would like to see people dancing around the room in a kind of West Pole version of the polka, or perhaps there will be a circle dance that snakes around the place, someone at the head of it waving one of my grandmother's tatted hankies. Even a man could do it just like it's done in Greece.

I hope the dark shadowed spector will walk with me hand in hand down dappled forested paths, redwood duff crunching underfoot. I'd like to travel past my favorite West Pole places before moving on.

The Bermuda Triangle of Us

Have you ever noticed that certain roads, highways and byways mark the boundaries of your life? My growing up years were spent traversing the Santa Ana and Hollywood freeways and the Pacific Coast Highway. Mill Valley signaled the Golden Gate Bridge, and Blithedale Avenue. But in the West County it's Coleman Valley Road, Joy Road, Bohemian Highway, Occidental Road and especially the Bodega Highway, that map my adventures at the West Pole.

Bodega Highway is not named for a wine warehouse as you might think, but after the Peruvian-Spanish explorer, Juan Francisco de la Bodega. Here it's a short run that connects Sebastopol to the coast. It might seem a slow, lazy stretch of road, except for the fact that it's the main route to the beaches and packed with cars during the hot summers, or even on cool foggy coastal days. The pull of the ocean. A tidal thing.

I've memorized this westward stretch of Bodega Highway— cattle grazing on softly-sculpted hills, a generous muddy pond, the curves that snake alongside Salmon Creek with its thick stands of water-loving willows. In late January, the willows are a garnet shade of deep purple red, sap rising; in March, they're rust-colored and covered in fuzzy white catkins. Harbingers of spring.

Scattered farmhouses dot the landscape. I always look for the one on the north side of the highway that was featured in the film *Phenomenon* starring John Travolta.

Non-native Scotch broom and gorse blossom a strong Hansa yellow in early spring. The troublesome non-native shrubs have invaded a lot of hilly pasture land. Sheep's wool gets caught on the gorse leaves, really inch long thorns, and small clumps of fur wave on the sea breezes as I drive by. Fingerling's of fog drift over the hilltops and signal the weather report for the beach: cool and damp. Sweatshirt with hoodie required.

When ranchers clear their pastures of manure, I travel the road with the windows rolled up tight. When I get home, the stench smelling like soured cheese and porta-potty permeates the air.

Driving further west, redwoods give way to oily eucalyptus. The scent of the trees somewhere between cat pee and Vicks Vapo-rub. Imported from Australia, eucalyptus is still used for windbreaks. There is a noticeably large burned patch in the grove where a live wire went down and started a big fire. The same one that burned our friend, Ben. Eucalyptus seed pods litter the old Bodega Calvary cemetery. Sometimes when I walk around in the cemetery reading names on old headstones, I pick up seed pods and study them—their centers like a little stars or little crosses—an echo of the crosses on the graves. The pods are a hippie remedy for fleas, and many times over the years I've threaded together the pods with a big thick needle and yarn for a dog flea collar, my fingers stinging with needle pricks afterwards.

But the collars never seemed that effective.

For over 28 years, Forrest and I have moved in a pattern, all connected to Bodega Highway. Forrest made a chart he calls "The Bermuda Triangle of Us."

Unlike the real triangle, planes and people don't disappear in our Bermuda Triangle, but there are shifts, and cracks.

There's one point on the triangle that leads to the past, to tales and stories, maybe changed to make us feel more benevolent, and another that portends the future, what we can only imagine. What disappears in this Bermuda Triangle of Us is time, and accurate memories.

Forrest circles an area on a Sonoma County map and then draws in the straight lines to complete a perfect triangle. This triangle connects the three houses we have lived in together. One point is on Bodega Highway The center point of the triangle lies somewhere within the mysteries of the deeply shaded redwood forest.

"This must be our power spot," Forrest said, as we signed the papers on our current house, the lane lushly lined in early fall with pink naked ladies. Our place is just a short drive to Bodega Highway. Then further on down Bodega Highway we pass Freestone, the sweet aroma of sticky bun bread baking in the brick ovens of Wild Flour wafting on the sea breezes. Then we drive past the Watson School, gates closed at sunset, past where the Christo Running Fence once ran, and onto Highway 1. We continue driving out to the Pacific Ocean until we hit the right turn onto Coleman Valley Road, winding, winding, around past Ocean Song, past the Wheeler Ranch, Bill Wheeler driving his truck loaded with paintings through the gate, past Star Mountain, down the hill into the heart of the West Pole, where we sit on the patio of the Union Hotel sipping Blue Moon beer as we watch the sky turn to mauve. We know that over the hill, the sun is sinking into the Pacific.

The Fool

Pull a card from the Tarot deck.
Find the fool,
all motley belongings knotted into a scarf,
tied to a stick.
His little dog barks to show him
that he's about to step off a cliff.
He's so filled with visons
he can't see where he's going.
He only knows he carries a rose in one hand
and his purpose
is to dream while awake,
to discover the impossible, to wander.

Calling All Fools

A llama, dressed in four rainbow-colored tutus starts off the parade. Two black and red-clad stilt walkers dance to the music of the wacky Hubbub Club Marching Band. The band's blaring brass, high pitched fiddles, thumpa thumpa drums, and ring-tone Glockenspiel reverberate into the Occidental hills.

As the stilt walkers tower above me, I try to snap pictures of the passing parade of fools. More fools in their motleys pass by, and then more jesters holding dogs on leashes. Pets are everywhere in the parade this year.

"Calling all fools, calling all fools," a woman with an old fashioned phone chatters away to a non-existent party, severed phone cord dangling. A nun walks by with the local choir. Her sign: "I make a habit of singing."

The stop sign in town says, "Flop" instead of "Stop," and where the Bohemian Highway was waterlogged just last week before spring finally sprung, a sign has been switched to read "Fooled" instead of "Flooded." It's time for the sillies—all of us April fools—to come out of our houses, out of the trees and parade through town. No mistaking it, it's that first Saturday in April in the West Pole.

This year there's no theme. I kind of miss last year's "Fin and Feathers" theme with one spectacular entry—six people carrying crepe paper covered poles that held together a fanciful rectangular aquarium filled with dangling paper and plastic fish. There were people dressed as fish and carrying fish cutouts that they swam up and down inside the paper water. A giant human jelly fish brought up the rear. But this year, as every year, we have the Luna Pillar. Created for Burning Man, pulled by a motorcyle, luna carries lots of kids and a few parents. Covered in flowers—mostly bright blues and turquoise, but with some pinks and yellows the scheme fits Jeff and Lisa. They built Luna and are dressed in the emerald shades of Oz year round.

The parade weaves along the Bohemian Highway and onto Main Street. Two adult-sized foxes hold hands and march along to fife and fiddle music just behind the Morris Dancers with jangling bells. A few rows behind are guys playing what look like homemade goatskin bag-  pipes. They're wearing kilts, a not unusual everyday attire around the West County. "The men in skirts," as daughter Grace calls them.

My husband Forrest comes by with two of our grandchildren. They're not in costume, although my granddaughter wears a white mask over her mouth and nose, looking scarily, like a victim of Japan's recent triple troubles: earthquake, tsunami, nuclear disaster. But really, she stops to tell me, she has something on her nose like a cold sore that she doesn't want anyone to notice. Forrest wears my jester hat which sparkles with stars and moons in silver and black, his nod to foolishness. I'm watching from the sidelines before dashing over the hill to an art opening in Bodega Bay. I can't really get out of it; I'm one of the featured artists. I'm sorry too because I love this crazy parade. I'm in my art opening costume, and while it's quirky and colorful, it can't match the enthusiastic color spree of the parading fools.

Last year I was here with my daughter Mary Lea and the grandkids were Batman and Fairy, a dynamic duo, with Bubby complaining that he couldn't see that well out of his mask. We didn't march, but watched. The year before that Forrest donned a lion mask and I wore all black with my black cat mask and tail. We held hands and smiled. Cat family.

But that was two years ago. This year my ex-husband, Scott suddenly pops up in front of me, wants to take my picture. I notice he has on the same shirt made of African fabric, brought back from Ghana, that our daughter Rowan has also given Forrest. I smile into the camera. We're friendly now; we've gotten over the past. I've gone to his recent wedding.

The woman next to me wears a leafy beaded dress and her eyes are covered by a leather green mask, "Hand made," her boy-friend tells me. She looks exotic, but she's not in the parade either, just a bystander. I think I recognize her as a local blues singer. Hard to tell today, everyone has chosen a different personae. Today Occidental resembles a Renaissance village. The Druids are happy today. The pagans, the ritual lovers—all happy. There's music and dancing and silly fools everywhere, and now, cameras and  film crews and TV cameras to record it all. The Fool's Day Parade has been "discovered."

This is the first year that there are more people watching than in the parade. The economic crises and bad-news-as-usual mentality are left in the dust, as the fools in this little town don't really take anything seriously today. This parade is a mixture of fleshy folk, breasts oozing out of costumes, men in tights, and bright colors. Charlie Chaplin, last year's prom queen driven in an old convertable, is a shop keeper in town. There's a beekeeper, and a big daddy bee with a baby boy bee on his hip. A carpenter, and single dad, I recognize the bee as a sometimes quilter from the Bodega quilting bee.

Tai chi fan dancers and musicians of all sorts glide by. Even a guy who will tell you a joke if you just pull on his thumb. There's music everywhere and laughter. A small town celebration.

The Fool's Day Parade, first started by Ramon Sender, known as Zero the Clown, has been coming to life on and off for the 35 years I've lived here. When Kate Price, a musician, but a fool by avocation, moved here, and started what she thought was a wonderful new idea, a Fools Parade, people told her, "Great idea, an April Fool's Parade. It's kind of been a tradition in Occidental; we'll march!" She called together the community with artsy signs of fools and gathered her motleys and clowns via email to join in the tumult. And now the local arts center has taken on the task of managing the unmanageable.

Last year some foolish women climbed onto the roof of the vintage clothing store and the women, clad in their own colorful bustiers, tulle skirts, fish net hose, and boots, tossed down women's undergarments. Lacy panties and bras rained down on the dancing crowd.

Our British friend Susan holds up an ornate butterfly mask as she struts by. She was once Forrest's girlfriend. Then there are the families who just grabbed things from their closets and march proudly with the others. They are into the spirit of the day, of the moment.

Occidental is a town of creative dreamers. The inventor of the Palm Pilot lives here, the founders of the Maker Faire. Masters of technology, founders of communes, of rock, of the blues, of going green and organic, call this home. Residents have gotten rich from cleverness, including blowing glass medical marijuana pipes, writing self-help books and murder mysteries. Or perhaps they sew, paint, sculpt, or play drums in a somewhat (or, perhaps, very) famous band. They save salmon and owls and lagunas and build a big garden at the elementary school that helps feed the kids at lunchtime. They have visions of how things should be.

I try to sort out the mystical meaning of such a parade in such a town. Occidental, the West Pole. The place where the tectonic plates collide. Where things slide down into the salty Pacific abyss. Where old hippies and new hippies, generations of hippies, mix with executives and just plain folk to walk foolishly together and say to the world, "We haven't any cares, we're all for new beginnings and we walk together in fun, not for any cures to cancer or for the cause of peace, but simply for the sheer exuberance of making fools of ourselves."

If he's watching, The Fool would approve. Right at home, he might stumble into place behind the Hubbub Club Marching Band, little dog nipping at his heels, and wander along fully satisfied to dream. And I'd be right behind him, feeling a little foolish, but stepping in tune to the tuba, the glockenspiel, and making my way, forever, without a compass at the West Pole.

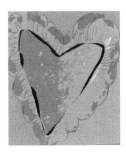

Acknowledgements

Special thanks to my editor Susan Bono.

Thank you to *The Pils*, who explored the West Pole with me:
Susan Swartz, Barbara Baer, and Robin Beeman.

Early editors and readers:
Bob Burnett, Suze Cohan, Roger Collins, Michael Dooley,
Patrick Fanning, Mary Gaffney, Emil Gonzalez, Roger
House, Lowell Martin, Judith Moorman, Salli Rasberry,
and Bart Schneider.

Editing and proofing: Roger House.
Cover and logo design: Jennifer Beckham.
Book design: Jo-Anne Rosen, Wordrunner Press.
For the suggestion of the Chinese proverb:
Thanks to Lowell Martin.
For the suggestion of a book: Thanks to Heidi Morgan.
For moral support and art advice: Thanks to Diane Senia.

With eternal gratitude to my family, especially daughters,
Anne, Amanda, Laurel, and step sons Jesse and Kyle, and
to their spouses, and to my grandchildren, Skyler, Sadira,
Saben Jr., Sol, and Jayden.
To my siblings Diane Matthews and Sam Downing, and my
sister-in-law Paula.

And to all the big tribe we've become throughout the years, including our ex's and their families.

Special thanks to the Dueñas: I couldn't imagine closer or more dedicated friends.
And with thanks and deep appreciation to all the friends residing both inside and outside the West Pole.

About the Author

Dreamer, artist, and descendent of explorers, Marylu Downing is a quirky native Californian who has made western Sonoma County her home for over 36 years. She is a retired college counselor who has raised three daughters and two step sons at the West Pole. Her writing has been published in many anthologies, in print media and online. Her art may be viewed at www.studioml.com.

Made in the USA
San Bernardino, CA
02 November 2013